Connected

Also by Peter Wallace

Living Loved
Out of the Quiet
TruthQuest Devotional Journal
Psalms for Today
What Jesus Is Saying to You Today
What God Is Saying to You Today
What the Psalmist Is Saying to You Today

Connected

You and God in the Psalms

Peter M. Wallace

MP Morehouse Publishing

NEW YORK · HARRISBURG · DENVER

Morehouse Publishing, 4775 Linglestown Road, Harrisburg, PA 17112
Morehouse Publishing, 445 Fifth Avenue, New York, NY 10016
Morehouse Publishing is an imprint of Church Publishing Incorporated.

Cover photo © by Michael Seufer www.weitesland.info
Author photo by Simon Cowart
Cover design by Jennifer Glosser

Library of Congress Cataloging-in-Publication Data

Wallace, Peter M.
    Connected : you and God in the Psalms / by Peter Marsden Wallace.
        p.   cm.
    ISBN 978-0-8192-2308-1 (pbk.)
    1. Bible. O.T. Psalms–Devotional use. 2. Spirituality–Biblical teaching. I. Title.
BS1430.54.W35   2009
242'.5–dc22
                                                                2009005949

Printed in the United States of America

09 10 11 12 13 14   10 9 8 7 6 5 4 3 2 1

Contents

Foreword   xi

Introduction   1

Delighted (Psalm 1)   6

Lifted (Psalm 3)   8

Disturbed (Psalm 4)   10

Awed (Psalm 8)   12

Obligated (Psalm 10)   14

Watched (Psalm 11)   16

Fooled (Psalm 14)   18

Included (Psalm 15)   20

Directed (Psalm 16)   22

Distressed (Psalm 18)   24

Messaged (Psalm 19)   26

Devastated (Psalm 22)   28

Protected (Psalm 23)   30

Soaked (Psalm 24)   32

Shamed (Psalm 25)   34

Vindicated (Psalm 26)   36

Afraid (Psalm 27)   38

Carried (Psalm 28)   40

Overwhelmed (Psalm 29)   42

Abandoned (Psalm 31)   44

Forgiven (Psalm 32)   46

Answered (Psalm 34)   48

Loved (Psalm 36)   50

Committed (Psalm 37)   52

Measured (Psalm 39)   54
Conflicted (Psalm 41)   56
Parched (Psalm 42)   58
Changed (Psalm 46)   60
Overjoyed (Psalm 47)   62
Possessed (Psalm 49)   64
Summoned (Psalm 50)   66
Cleansed (Psalm 51)   68
Rooted (Psalm 52)   70
Betrayed (Psalm 55)   72
Delivered (Psalm 56)   74
Awakened (Psalm 57)   76
Angered (Psalm 58)   78
Staggered (Psalm 60)   80
Sheltered (Psalm 61)   82
Silenced (Psalm 62)   84
Watered (Psalm 65)   86
Tested (Psalm 66)   88
Blessed (Psalm 67)   90
Strengthened (Psalm 68)   92
Mired (Psalm 69)   94
Surrounded (Psalm 70)   96
Nurtured (Psalm 71)   98
Reminded (Psalm 74)   100
Troubled (Psalm 77)   102
Guided (Psalm 78)   104
Restored (Psalm 80)   106
Satisfied (Psalm 81)   108
Nested (Psalm 84)   110
Turned (Psalm 85)   112
Wholehearted (Psalm 86)   114
Refreshed (Psalm 87)   116
Shunned (Psalm 88)   118
Counted (Psalm 90)   120
Covered (Psalm 91)   122

Launched (Psalm 92)   124
Celebrated (Psalm 95)   126
Judged (Psalm 98)   128
Refocused (Psalm 100)   130
Integrated (Psalm 101)   132
Wasted (Psalm 102)   134
Freed (Psalm 103)   136
Welcomed (Psalm 104)   138
Encouraged (Psalm 105)   140
Stressed (Psalm 107)   142
Infuriated (Psalm 109)   144
Wised Up (Psalm 111)   146
Raised (Psalm 113)   148
Shakened (Psalm 114)   150
Distracted (Psalm 115)   152
Cherished (Psalm 116)   154
Determined (Psalm 119)   156
Kept (Psalm 121)   158
Surrounded (Psalm 125)   160
Rewarded (Psalm 126)   162
Doubtful (Psalm 128)   164
Pardoned (Psalm 130)   166
Quieted (Psalm 131)   168
United (Psalm 133)   170
Remembered (Psalm 136)   172
Wonderfully Made (Psalm 139)   174
Championed (Psalm 140)   176
Guarded (Psalm 141)   178
Happy (Psalm 146)   180
Brokenhearted (Psalm 147)   182
Enthused (Psalm 150)   184

Endnotes   187
Index   191

Acknowledgments

The author wishes to express his deep appreciation to his editor, Cynthia Shattuck, and the staff at Church Publishing; to Skip Schueddig and the team at *Day1* and the Alliance for Christian Media; to his family and friends who are such an encouragement; to Michael Seufer for his friendship and photography; to Greg Garrett; and to Danh Le.

Foreword

by Greg Garrett

L ast week I was teaching the psalms in a graduate seminar on grief and suffering in literature. I asked the class how they had encountered the psalms
before our formal study together, and the answers were pretty typical. One
student talked about being raised Catholic, hearing the psalms chanted in
liturgy, and basically ignoring them Sunday after Sunday. Another talked
about how a hand-picked set of psalms had been a part of her devotional
reading, reinforcing ideas about God's goodness and blessing. And one of my
students, God bless him, raised his hand and confessed, "I've never really
been able to connect with the psalms. Most of them, I mean. I've lived a
really happy life. Nothing bad has ever happened to me. I've never felt persecuted, or hopeless, or near death."

"Okay," I said, and we moved on, although inwardly I was thinking, "Oh,
honey. Enjoy it while you can."

Because, although I fear this does violence to both Psalms 1 and 23,
happy indeed is the one who has not walked through the valley of the
shadow of death.

Lucky, in fact.

Fortunate.

And while of course I don't wish my student ill—or any of those fortunate ones who have walked through life so far resonating only with the
psalms of praise—we know that eventually all of us will know suffering and
trial because that is the nature of life, a truth the psalmists knew, clearly,
from experience. As Thomas Cahill writes, the psalms are perhaps our earliest example of literature with an "I" connected, of interior wrestling, of
writers on an emotional journey in the presence of the Living God. The
psalms, he says, are a "treasure trove of personal emotions from poets acutely
attuned to their inner states, from ancient harpists dramatically aware that
spirit calls to Spirit—that their pain and joy can find permanent satisfaction
only in the Creator of all."[1]

I know a little something about these things myself, pain, and joy, and
satisfaction in the Creator. Unlike my student, I have felt persecuted, hope-

---

1. Thomas Cahill, *The Gifts of the Jews* (New York: Anchor, 1998), 198–99.

less, or near death, and like many who have faced one or more of these situations, the psalms spoke to me when almost nothing else did—or could. In weary years when life seemed too difficult to go on living, Psalm 27, a psalm of David, often came to my lips, a repeated hope of connection to God despite everything:

> The LORD is my light and my salvation;
>   whom shall I fear?
> The LORD is the stronghold of my life;
>   of whom shall I be afraid?
> (Ps. 27:1, NRSV)

And my experience echoes the experience of other souls, whether faithful or searching, for thousands of years. As Robert Alter notes in his introduction to his own recent translation of the psalms, these verses of Hebrew praise and lament have been at the foundation of Jewish and Christian life, "the most urgently, personally present of all the books of the Bible in the lives of many readers."[2] It is this knowledge of the personal power of the psalms that Peter Wallace carries into the book that you are holding, a book that attempts to strengthen and broaden our experience of the psalms so that they will continue to speak to us today.

Peter Wallace understands the power of the psalms, and the need to engage them—all of them, praise and lament and confusion alike. Through the use of his own experience—his own inner life—he opens up each of the psalms for us so that we can see them anew, while in his concluding prayers for each section, he acknowledges the difficulty of many of these texts, the trials in many of our lives—and the ongoing goodness of God.

Ultimately, the psalms are about connecting to God, in good times and in bad, when we see hope shining everywhere and when we are in the valley of the shadow. Peter's strong and consistent focus on connection makes this book one to be savored and returned to. I hope it will highlight that connection for you and draw you into the knowledge that, as Peter writes in one of his prayers, God is still our place of refuge:

Thank you for being the exalted God who knows and acts and is. Thank you that in the midst of a world of change, you are the changeless One.

Happy is the one who knows this.
Fortunate, even.

Greg Garrett
Baylor University
Austin, Texas

---

2. Robert Alter, *The Book of Psalms* (New York: W. W. Norton, 2007), xiii.

Introduction

Rio de Janeiro is an astonishing city. Everywhere you look, in any direction, you see something beautiful. Or surprising. Or funny. Or frightening. Or overwhelming.

The city is surrounded by wide, clean beaches—Leblon, Ipanema, Copacabana—crowded with sun worshippers of all shapes, sizes, ages, nationalities, and backgrounds. The urban center is populated by uniquely Brazilian modern architecture, including the Catedral de Sao Sebastian, a pyramid-shaped skyscraper that literally takes your breath away when you walk into its soaring sanctuary.

Wherever you turn in Rio, you see massive jungle-shrouded mountains jutting into the sky at odd angles, including the famous Sugarloaf Mountain and the Corcovado—home of one of the most impressive and inspiring religious statues in the world: Cristo Redentor, Christ the Redeemer, who towers over all with his arms outstretched in graceful invitation.

Just as I was starting to write this book, I had the opportunity to spend a couple of weeks in Brazil on vacation with my friend Dan. My world travels so far have been somewhat limited, but in each case the culture and environment I found myself in quickly absorbed me, filling me with enthusiasm.

But before I left for Brazil, I can't tell you how many people warned me to be careful in Rio. The crime, they told me, was pervasive. Perhaps that set my expectations on a negative path.

Even so, I thoroughly enjoyed the time in Rio, as well as our visit to the falls at Iguazu National Park toward the end of the trip. There was a good bit of sightseeing, shopping, eating, and hanging out at the beach. Yet I realized something unusual about my experience in Brazil. I began keeping track of the emotions I felt. And they were all over the map.

As I paid closer attention to my emotions, I found my mind gravitating to the book of Psalms. What struck me was that all the emotions I was feeling in Brazil echoed the feelings so clearly expressed in the psalms.

Somehow, the writers of these songs in the Hebrew Bible were able to identify and express their emotions—whatever they were—and relate them to their experience of God in prayer and meditation. That's exactly what I found myself doing in Brazil.

- The awe of creation that constantly surrounded me—the lush green hills, the rolling sea, the intensely blazing sunsets behind ragged green mountains—and the joy of seeing colorful birds and reptiles in a Bird Park near Iguazu Falls, and the wild range of flowers and luxuriant foliage in Rio's Jobim Botanical Garden . . .

When I look at your heavens, the work of your fingers, the moon and the stars that you have established; what are human beings that you are mindful of them, mortals that you care for them? (Ps. 8:3–4)

- The fear I often felt walking the streets of Rio, especially after an unfortunate run-in with a tattoo artist on the beach who kept trying to extort money from me, even threatening me with death . . .

The LORD is my light and my salvation; whom shall I fear? The LORD is the stronghold of my life; of whom shall I be afraid? (Ps. 27:1)

- The powerful waterfalls of Iguazu that surrounded me, shaking the very foundation of the earth under my feet . . .

God is our refuge and strength, a very present help in trouble. Therefore we will not fear, though the earth should change, though the mountains shake in the heart of the sea; though its waters roar and foam, though the mountains tremble with its tumult. (Ps. 46:1–3)

- The questions and doubts that arose when considering the abject poverty that butts up right against the wealth of the beautiful people— crumbling favelas on lush hillsides not far from exclusive gated neighborhoods—the inequity, power struggles, and fears that arise from that class conflict and the desperate needs of poverty . . .

People will say, "Surely there is a reward for the righteous; surely there is a God who judges on earth." (Ps. 58:11)

- The uncertainties of making the flight connections, of making my way through complicated security and customs lines, of finding my way to the right place and not getting lost, of not having a clue about the language . . .

Then they cried to the LORD in their trouble, and he delivered them from their distress; he led them by a straight way, until they reached an inhabited town. (Ps. 107:6–7)

On and on the emotions flowed, and the songs of the faithful would come to mind, giving me the encouragement or insight I was yearning to discover and express and make my own. And in the months after that sojourn in Brazil, I have found myself walking through everyday life with very similar emotions but in very different circumstances. Yet the psalms continue to enable me both to express my deep feelings to God and to find spiritual nourishment in the midst of them.

The psalms can help us make solid connections with our own feelings and with God, connections that enable us to better live a full and meaningful life. And when we strengthen those connections, then we can connect to other people in ever wider circles, in the community of faith and then into the world that yearns for true connection with God. That's the purpose of this spiritual journey through the book of Psalms.

What Are the Psalms?

The book of Psalms is a collection of prayers and songs used in worship and meditation by the Israelites, written probably between 1000 and 300 BCE. They aren't dry history or pedantic teaching. They seem to breathe with life, helping us to connect to the living God who was and is and is to come.

In a review of a new translation of the Psalms, which critic James Wood calls "the noisiest book in the Hebrew Bible," Wood writes: "The Book of Psalms is the great oasis in which a desert people gathers to pour out its complaints, fears, hopes; the Psalms are prayers, songs, incantations, and perhaps even soliloquies. In them, the supplicants invoke God as their light, their water, their warrior, their scourge, their buckler, their rod, and their staff."[1] Psalms reveal, "again and again, the gap between our language and the indescribable God, between our certainty that God is with us and our anxiety that he has abandoned us, between his cosmic proportions and our comic littleness."[2]

I've found the psalms to be an almost visceral, flesh and blood expression of authentic emotion and deep faith. As Debbie Blue puts it, "The psalmist has a body, and it figures prominently in his poetry. His kidneys lash him, his heart rejoices, his pulse (or liver) beats with joy. His body is not gross matter imprisoning him; it pulsates, breathes, dwells securely and participates fully in the overflowing joy and delight he feels in God's right hand forever. Heart-pulse-body-flesh-joy-delight. It's sweat and skin and secretions more than white gloves, church pews and Easter bonnets."[3]

Fred R. Anderson, pastor of Madison Avenue Presbyterian Church in New York City, paraphrased in an interview with me something his professor of Old Testament Theology at Princeton Seminary, Bernhard W. Anderson, said while teaching a course on Psalms: "There's going to come a time when you find yourself dry and that's the time you need to go to the well of the Psalms, which have nurtured the faithful for eons. When you find yourself in that place, go to the Psalter and start praying it; not reading it, praying it. . . . This book is going to be your source of sustenance."4

I've found that to be true in my life. If you haven't yet, you will.

For all these reasons and many more, the book of Psalms has provided countless people of faith of all ages with unique spiritual resources for worship, praise, and growth. The psalms are living and breathing, and they open the door for us to live and breathe as authentic children of God—people who are honest with ourselves, with God, and with others, about our problems, our feelings, our needs, and our dreams. Psalms invite the sort of openness and honesty we need to be God's people in this world at this time.

Using This Book

I've written meditations based on the psalms before. *What the Psalmist Is Saying to You Today* (later revised as *Psalms for Today* using a different Bible translation) was a page-a-day book with chunks of what I hope were inspiring and illuminating thoughts on a verse or two. That was a long time ago—a whole lifetime ago it seems. And those devotionals were brief and impersonal.

Now I've been given the opportunity to return to the psalms and explore their meaning anew, to grapple with them more authentically and personally in the place I am now, through the lens of a faith that's a bit scarred and travel-weary but more rich and real than ever.

So in this book you'll find a lot of stories about me and other people I know or have read about as they work through the rough patches of life, deal with doubts and fears, learn lessons the hard way, experience surprising joy, and above all seek God's presence, protection, and promise in their lives.

I've tried to write these meditations so that whoever you are, you can see yourself in them. You may be a student in high school, a young adult just starting out in your career, a parent trying to find some sustenance in the midst of a crazy schedule, or someone who, like me, has a few miles on them. Perhaps you've believed in God your whole life long or are just starting to explore the spiritual side of life. No matter. I truly hope you feel at home here.

We'll explore together 90 of the 150 psalms. You can read these chapters straight through, or dip into them wherever you choose. And each chapter has been tagged with several themes and topics, so if you're looking for insight on particular issues or needs in your own life, use the index to find relevant meditations.

Please take your time reading the excerpts I've provided from the psalms, which are taken from the New Revised Standard Version of the Bible. And let the thoughts I've shared in these pages spur your own thinking, remind you of events in your life, and open the door to appropriate responses and actions. At the end of each chapter is a prayer, which I hope will serve as a starting point for your own conversation with God.

As you read these meditations on the psalms, I pray that you find yourself connected more deeply and securely to yourself, to the God who loves you, to your fellow pilgrims in faith, and to the world in need around you.

Peter Wallace
Atlanta, Georgia
February 2009

Delighted

Psalm 1

THEMES
Peer Pressure
Bible
Happiness
Fellowship
Meaning

If you're going to get anywhere you really want to end up being, you have to start moving in the right direction, on the right path.

Of course, you know how tough it is not only to choose that path—to figure out which of many that may lie before you is the best one to take—but then to stay on it. There are a lot of people in your life—at work, in your classes, at your fitness center, next door, online, wherever—who want you to join them on a path that may not go anywhere except into trouble or pain or emptiness.

They may mean well. And there's nothing wrong with having fun and exploring life, even taking a risk. But you know in your gut what's right for you, what's positive, what will make your life meaningful and happy in the long run. You know, deep down, what may be entertaining for a while but will end up only leaving you messed up. With a broken heart. Or with somebody's hurt feelings you have to make right. Or maybe with a dented fender, or at least a headache. Or worse.

The writer of the first psalm makes it plain and simple:

> *1 Happy are those who do not follow the advice of the wicked,*
> *or take the path that sinners tread, or sit in the seat of scoffers;*

Of course, you'd never call some of the people in your life wicked or sinners or scoffers. But you know that feeling you get when somebody suggests doing something you doubt would be good and healthy for you. It's anything but happy.

Even so, sometimes when we're struggling with boredom or sensing a lack of meaning or motivation in life, or we get tired of our routine, we let ourselves get drawn down a path that leads to trouble and hurt. Without thinking it through, we jump at any opportunity to relieve our exhausting monotony—with sometimes surprisingly tragic results.

Picking the wrong path has been the plot line of a number of motion pictures in recent years. One of the best is *After Hours*, directed by Martin Scorsese. Paul, our "hero," is a lonely, bored computer consultant. He wastes his evenings watching TV and simply passing time until, one night, he decides to get out and do something, anything.

At a nearby coffee shop he meets an attractive but somewhat bizarre woman. Later he calls her, she invites him over, and terrifying hilarity ensues. Moving from one misadventure to another caused by multiple calamities, mistaken identities, and some really stupid decisions, Paul manages to survive a hellish night. At one point he says, "I just wanted to leave my apartment, maybe meet a nice girl, and now I've got to die for it?"

In the end, Paul gets dumped in front of his office building at the start of the next workday. And life goes on.

Well, this scenario of choosing the wrong path may make for some interesting films, but it's not much fun in real life.

So why not be your own person, go where you want to go—where you feel called to go? Why not choose to do something positive instead of following the herd mentality or doing something stupid just for the thrill of it? You're not a lemming, you're a unique child of God.

You can choose another path, one that promises meaning and delight in life—one that God promises is not as pathetic as some may think:

2 . . . their delight is in the law of the LORD, and on his law they meditate day and night.

If you're involved in a church or small group, you're probably already involved in some kind of personal exploration of God's word. And, good for you, you're reading this book! The point is, get some positive input. Get connected with God. Stimulate your mind and heart with spiritual insights and ideas. And do it with other people who care about you.

And when you get advice or an invitation you find yourself wrestling with, listen to your inner self. Listen to God's Spirit within you. You can say "no," you know. You can change your mind at any point you find yourself down the wrong path. You really are that strong.

You'll find that the more you walk this way . . .

- the more you'll see all the pieces of your life making some sense, working together to form something good and meaningful;
- the more you can trust God to work out the messy things in your life— or the more you can accept them as reality and not worth getting so freaked out about;
- the more the psalmist's promise can come true for you:

3 They are like trees planted by streams of water, which yield their fruit in its season, and their leaves do not wither. In all that they do, they prosper.

Sounds delightful, doesn't it? Keep on this path and you've got a truly exciting life in front of you.

God, let's be honest. I like having fun. I enjoy my friends and, yes, sometimes I make decisions that aren't as positive and wise as they could be. But I don't want to get stuck there. I want to be moving in the right direction. I want to be filling my head with the good stuff. Your stuff. I want to end up growing like that fruit tree by the water stream. I want to thrive. And I want you to be as delighted with my life as I am.

Lifted

Fear
Safety
Security
Protection
Deliverance
Trouble
Anxiety

1 O LORD, how many are my foes! Many are rising against me;

2 many are saying to me, "There is no help for you in God."

Maybe you're paranoid, but sometimes it seems there are an awful lot of people out to get you. You just try to get along, take care of yourself, do the right thing. But everywhere you turn, there's an obstacle. And if not an obstacle, an enemy. Someone or something that seems designed to sidetrack you, or worse, take you down.

A friend of mine had an experience that felt an awful lot like that to him. At his company, a better position opened at another branch office much closer to his home. He was ready for a change and more responsibility, and besides, while he got along fine with his co-workers and his supervisor, he had always felt a bit of a strain with some of them.

When word got around that he had become a finalist for the promotion, he told me it felt like the knives came out against him. At least one of his colleagues had also applied for the job, unsuccessfully, and she convinced others that my friend had cheated somehow to win consideration. Suddenly, odd things started happening at work. Some of his paperwork was lost. Computer files got scrambled. Even his supervisor seemed to be in on the act, leaning on him to get more done. He thought he was losing his mind. Was it all a coincidence, or were they really out to get him?

In times like those we have to remind ourselves, like the psalmist, about the character and actions of the God we want to be connected to:

3 But you, O LORD, are a shield around me, my glory, and the one who lifts up my head. . . .

When you find yourself feeling overwhelmed by people who want to hurt you, here are things to remember about the God who loves you:

- God surrounds you with protection. God's shield is not just in front of you, but all around you;
- God is your glory—the source of all that is good and pure and strong and bright in your life;
- God's hands hold your downcast face and turn it up to the light, enabling you to look beyond the dark and troubling circumstances to see the light of love and security.

And this is what happens when you let God be God in your life:

*5 I lie down and sleep; I wake again, for the L*ORD *sustains me.*

6 I am not afraid of ten thousands of people who have set themselves against me all around.

Life is filled with little skirmishes of the heart, mind, and soul. And some of them are not so little. Maybe you are a little paranoid. But the reality is that if you're going to move forward through the temptations and the pains and the messy parts of life, you need to let God lift your head. So you can see where God is taking you.

God, I don't want to live life scared, suspicious, anxious. I don't want to keep my head down, weighed by fear, afraid of what I'll see. I want to wrap you around me, knowing that you are protecting me, asking you to open my eyes and lift my gaze so I can take a realistic view of the situation, unhindered by anxiety or misunderstanding. I want to lie down and sleep in the assurance that you are with me no matter what people, or life, or the world throw at me. And thank you, with all my heart, for the lift.

Disturbed

THEMES

Accusations

Anger

Shame

Lies

Hurts

Forgiveness

Justice

¹ Answer me when I call, O God of my right! You gave me room when I was in distress. Be gracious to me, and hear my prayer.

² How long, you people, shall my honor suffer shame? How long will you love vain words, and seek after lies? . . .

Right smack in the middle of a hectic day my cell phone rang. The caller ID informed me an old friend was on the line, one I hadn't talked with for some time because we'd both been so busy. I answered gladly. But instead of hearing a pleasant greeting, a harsh accusation assaulted my ear: "Hey," my friend challenged me, "what gives you the right to tell people about my DUI last summer?"

It took me a few seconds to figure out what he was charging me with, but I could feel my face burning red from shock and embarrassment, as well as anger, because the accusation was false. And I got right back into his face about it.

After a very uncomfortable conversation, we both calmed down a bit and talked it through. Ultimately he understood what must have happened: Somebody took what I'd said about a DUI arrest I'd read about in the news and spread it around, until it came back around to my friend. Because the circumstances were similar, he'd assumed it was his story that had been spread around. And I must have been the one who started it because I was the only friend who knew about it. Of course, as a result of his angry misunderstanding, he had let people know about the situation he had been trying so hard to keep secret.

The psalmist had a similar problem with people's unfounded accusations, but the stakes were far higher. He was the victim of humiliating lies spread around by people who wanted to hurt him, who wanted to knock him down a peg or two. It was infuriating. And he was angry.

So he demanded that God help him, as God had in the past: "You gave me room when I was in distress" (v. 1). He had felt hemmed in and overwhelmed before, and God had opened the way to relieve him. Now in the midst of his fury over this new injustice, he asked for God's help again.

But then the psalmist gave himself some very wise advice, which my friend and I would have done well to follow:

4 When you are disturbed [or angry], do not sin; ponder it on your beds, and be silent.

5 Offer right sacrifices, and put your trust in the LORD. . . .

You may have every right and reason to be disturbed, angry, and upset. But take a deep breath. Don't react out of that anger, as I did at first with my friend. Don't make it your aim to strike back at those who are hurting you, because you'll only get yourself into a deeper mess.

Instead, be quiet. Stay in silence. Think it through. Get a clear picture of what's happening. Make sure you know what the truth of the situation is, rather than jumping to conclusions or overreacting to your hurt.

Let the fury dissolve in the presence of God's Spirit. Let loose. Let go. Breathe deeply. Give it some space. And then do what's right. Trust God to work it out.

If you do that, you will avoid hurting yourself and anybody else. The situation will resolve itself whether through your calm words or actions, or some other way. And as a result the psalmist promises:

8 I will both lie down and sleep in peace; for you alone, O LORD, make me lie down in safety.

God, listen to me. It's not fair and it hurts. It's embarrassing. And it's a lie. There may be some truth to it, all right, but what will people think? Please hear me. Help me get clear. Give me room to breathe. Let me learn what I need to learn from all this, and make it right. Help me to live right, so that there's no chance that people will misunderstand me or jump to wild conclusions. I want to let go in your peace and hope. I want to live so that I know your joy.

11

Awed

Psalm 8

THEMES
Majesty
Creation
Responsibility
Dominion

I've been startled by stars on a number of occasions.

Late at night on a tropical island in the blue-green South China Sea off Thailand's mainland.

On a jungle-edged Costa Rican beach covered by dozens of two-foot-long Olive Ridley sea turtles laying their eggs in total darkness, driven only by instinct.

Even in an undeveloped forested area of North Georgia on a camping trip with my son.

I look up and see an astonishing array of glittering diamonds on black velvet—a breathtaking panorama far more spectacular than the meager night display typically seen in the city whose sky is drained by an overabundance of artificial light.

Where were you when the stars surprised you? How small did they make you feel? How overcome were you by the scale of reality?

And did you think of God? The psalmist did. And that quickly put things into perspective.

1 O LORD, our Sovereign, how majestic is your name in all the earth! You have set your glory above the heavens. . . .

3 When I look at your heavens, the work of your fingers, the moon and the stars that you have established;

4 what are human beings that you are mindful of them, mortals that you care for them?

You can't help but feel small under the weight of the starry night sky. And consider that the psalmist had no idea that the little pinpricks of light in the firmament were actually mammoth burning suns surrounded by countless planets and asteroids. Galaxies. Universes.

And here we are on our minuscule planet. Does God care? Does God even see us?

Once I watched countless people moving along the Ipanema Beach sidewalk outside my hotel window, and from my vantage point they looked like tiny ants. Walking, jogging, riding bikes, talking. Cars going every which way. I tried to look at some of these people individually, wondering who they were. Why were they right here right now? What were they thinking about, worrying over, frightened of, pleased about, hopeful for, tired of?

I hadn't a clue, of course. I could hardly see them. And I was only a few stories above them.

How does God do it? Why does God care?

I don't know, and I don't think the psalmist did either, but the psalmist was certain that God does care. And what's more, God expects us to care too.

5 Yet you have made them a little lower than God, and crowned them with glory and honor.

6 You have given them dominion over the works of your hands; you have put all things under their feet, . . .

We're responsible for this very creation, the world in which we live. But that word "dominion" has gotten humanity into a great deal of trouble for millennia. We think it gives us license to use the animal, vegetable, and mineral resources around us arrogantly, selfishly. Because we're in charge.

That's why we need to keep in mind the majestic perspective of the first part of this psalm. We're not in charge, God is. And God wants us to care for the works of God's hands. To conserve and protect and improve the natural resources. To do our part against drought and global warming and waste. It's the only reasonable response we can make.

9 O LORD, our Sovereign, how majestic is your name in all the earth!

Sometimes, God, you blow me away. When I take the time and make the effort to extend my focus beyond my own nose and see what's up in the sky and all around me, my brain explodes. The weight of your majesty and creativity overwhelms me. I feel so small. And then I realize that, even so, you know me totally. And you expect a lot from me. Open my eyes more often, God, so I can see not only the beauty of your creation, but also what I need to do to fulfill my responsibility toward it.

Obligated

THEMES
Poverty
Oppression
Pride
Prosperity
Hope
Helplessness
Justice

1 Why, O LORD, do you stand far off? Why do you hide yourself in times of trouble?

Those commercials get to me. You know the ones where some compassionate spokesperson walks down a muddy, rutty road in a favela or ghetto or somewhere I hope never to find myself, holding an impossibly sweet little girl wearing rags and no shoes, and begs us to call for a free information kit with a photo and biography of a child we could help educate and treat medically with a modest monthly donation.

The other day I watched one of these commercials and noticed that the spokesperson repeated the phrase "no obligation" several times, and the words were flashed on the screen. In other words, call for this free information. You don't have to pay anything now. Just check it out. There's no obligation. Really.

But isn't there?

The psalmist seemed to think so. And he thought it was God's obligation, and God wasn't fulfilling it.

2 In arrogance the wicked persecute the poor—let them be caught in the schemes they have devised. . . .

Not only are there poor people in need all around, but the wicked and the prosperous are persecuting them. They in effect deny God's love—and even God's existence—because if there were a God, surely such oppression would not exist.

4 In the pride of their countenance the wicked say, "God will not seek it out"; all their thoughts are, "There is no God." . . .

Admit it, you've wondered the same too. You see how people live, not only in the Third World, but in areas of your own town just a few miles away from you. You see starving children in Darfur and weak, sick people in India. You see workers slaving under oppressive conditions for pitiful pay to make products with high profit margins. You see victims of natural tragedies—fire, hurricane, tsunami, cyclone, tornado, earthquake, flood—wondering how in the world they can ever put the shattered pieces of their lives back together.

14

Doesn't it make you angry? Fill you with sadness and doubt? Doesn't it prompt you to join in the psalmist's cry:

12 Rise up, O Lord; O God, lift up your hand; do not forget the oppressed. . . .

You can also rest in the realization the psalmist had concerning the promise of God:

14 But you do see! Indeed you note trouble and grief, that you may take it into your hands; the helpless commit themselves to you; you have been the helper of the orphan. . . .

But how does God help in this world? Through God's people.

We are God's hands and feet. Out of the wealth of provision God has blessed us with, we are to share and provide and meet needs. Whether those needs are next door, across town, or in some far corner of the world. Whether it's through simple acts of service, delivering some meals, participating in a homeless shelter, or generous contributions to trustworthy organizations that provide care.

Because of our own situation, it may not be much. But that's more than enough in the power of the Spirit.

No obligation? No way.

17 O Lord, you will hear the desire of the meek; you will strengthen their heart, you will incline your ear

18 to do justice for the orphan and the oppressed, so that those from earth may strike terror no more.

Not out of guilt. Not out of anger. Not out of fear. But out of a sense of fulfilling your call on me, God, let me be part of the vast web of love and service around the world, caring for the poor, the oppressed, the hungry, the orphaned, in your name. Help me see what I can do, right now, today, to make a difference, to strengthen their hearts and do justice.

Watched

THEMES
Protection
Fear
Security
Righteousness

*1 In the LORD I take refuge; how can you say to me,
"Flee like a bird to the mountains;*

*2 for look, the wicked bend the bow, they have fitted
their arrow to the string, to shoot in the dark at the upright in heart.*

3 If the foundations are destroyed, what can the righteous do?"

For a time some years ago, I fantasized about running away. I let the scenario play out in my mind. I would throw a few things into a satchel, climb into my car, gas up, and hit the highway and drive as far as I could go. Maybe Key West–the end of the line. Or somewhere out West. I would find a cheap room to rent, get a job washing dishes somewhere, and spend my free time writing cheap novels. Surely that would get me out of the dead-end job I was in, the frustrations of the life I had woven for myself, the inauthenticity that imprisoned me. I would run away and start all over again.

Of course it never happened–that scenario anyway. I didn't "flee like a bird to the mountains," as the psalmist wrote, mocking the advice others had given him.

Oh, I would get away by myself, in the mountains of North Georgia or on the sandy beaches of St. Simons Island, for a few days of resting, reading, writing, meditating, even painting. Those were places of refuge, of safety, of renewal. But real life always insisted on roaring back, on sucking me back into it. And after a few precious days, I was back in the maelstrom, feeling much like the psalmist described. Arrows flew; some hit their target. How I wanted to run away again.

But slowly, inevitably, I came to the same conclusion the psalmist did: I took refuge in God. Because only in God is there utter safety and security, even in the midst of a shower of arrows. Fleeing like a bird to the mountains or the beach may help temporarily, but that's not going to change anything. You have to stay in it, deal with it, live as righteously, authentically, and lovingly as you can, and trust God.

After all, God sees and knows. Everything.

4 The LORD is in his holy temple; the LORD'S throne is in heaven. His eyes behold, his gaze examines humankind.

5 The LORD tests the righteous and the wicked, and his soul hates the lover of violence. . . .

7 For the LORD is righteous; he loves righteous deeds; the upright shall behold his face.

When we struggle to make a difficult decision, God watches.

When we do all we can to reconcile with a hurt family member or friend, God watches.

When we feel overcome by fear, whether real or imagined, God watches.

When we give in to pressures and handle problems in cruel or unfeeling ways, God watches.

When we face rejection or abandonment in an important relationship, God watches.

When we sacrifice something to make a positive difference, God watches.

When we wound someone out of our selfishness, God watches.

When we crack under pressure, God watches.

And God not only watches but reaches out in righteousness and love. When we're creative, God applauds. When we give of ourselves and our possessions, God enjoys it. When we're merciful, extending grace and forgiveness and trust to those who have hurt us, God cheers. When we're righteous, sharing God's identity, God absolutely loves it.

Stop trying to run away. Stop searching for a refuge like a bird fleeing to the mountains. Find your rest and your refuge in God, and behold how your life is transformed.

God, I hate it when the sharp arrows of life rain down on me in the dark. I just want to get away, to crawl in some hole somewhere or find some deserted island and start over. But I guess that's not what you've called me to. You want me to trust you, to find my safety and protection in you, in the midst of it all, and to live righteously. To be the person you created me to be, and to let your justice, love, and grace move through me. Let me begin today.

Fooled

Psalm 14

THEMES
Belief
Faith
Foolishness
Righteousness
Action
Wisdom

1 Fools say in their hearts, "There is no God." They are corrupt, they do abominable deeds; there is no one who does good.

In recent years there has been a surge of books by evangelizing atheists who claim that not only is there no God, but that belief in a God of any stripe is harmful. I wince at the good points these authors occasionally make, but I find their tone generally as self-satisfied and close-minded as extremists on the other end of the religious spectrum.

I subscribe to a weekly e-mail newsletter that includes the religious bestsellers list. In the past couple of years it has included a number of these books by atheists such as Richard Dawkins and Christopher Hitchens, which frankly strikes me as unfair. They're antireligious! Why should they be on the religious bestsellers list?

At such times I may try to take solace from Psalm 14:1, and consider those who reject God to be fools.

Foolishness in this case is not stupidity or even ignorance. It simply refers to one's decision to live apart from God, without faith in God, and the psalmist says it results in evil. Being wise doesn't necessarily mean being smarter, it's rather a commentary on one's choice to live in pursuit of God.

We all know which side we're on, don't we? It's a nice, smug, satisfying feeling, isn't it?

Until you keep reading.

2 The LORD looks down from heaven on humankind to see if there are any who are wise, who seek after God.

3 They have all gone astray, they are all alike perverse; there is no one who does good, no, not one.

Ouch.

There's a sense, the psalmist is saying, in which we're all fools. We're so caught up in our own needs and desires, our own dreams and goals, our own purposes and plans, that we live and act as if we are saying, deep within our hearts, "There is no God."

Believing in God, following God's will, is serious business. Yes, it's a matter of our heart, mind, and will, but it's also a matter of our hands and feet—doing something about what we believe, making a difference in the world by being God's hands and feet.

It's a matter of our tongue–building up rather than tearing down, bringing hope rather than fear, sharing insights rather than spreading gossip.

It's a matter of our wallet–putting our money where our mouth is. And not just our money, but also our time and talent.

So how wise are we really?

God, it's easy for me to point my finger and cluck my tongue at the fools who don't believe you're real. But rather than judging them, remind me to consider my own actions and motivations, and to ask myself, "If somebody looked at the way I lived, the words I said, and the plans I've made, would they consider me foolish or wise?"

Included

THEMES
Righteousness
Abiding
Truth
Relationships
Honesty
Belonging

1 O LORD, who may abide in your tent? Who may dwell on your holy hill?

In the film *Annie Hall*, Woody Allen's character Alvy Singer refers to an old Groucho Marx joke that describes his relationships with women: "I would never want to belong to any club that would have someone like me for a member."[5]

We all have a need to belong–not only to another person, other friends and families, but also to communities and groups. Especially faith communities.

Our relationship with God is rich and full and indescribable and often unbelievable, which only leads us to feel we don't truly belong there. So who are the "righteous"? What kind of person does belong in the presence of God? Who can be bold enough to enter the dwelling place of God? Who is permitted to bask in the glory of God's grace and love?

The psalmist struggled with this question: Who is worthy of membership in God's "club"?

In the next few verses, he provides some clues as to the kind of people God likes to be with. Who?

2a Those who walk blamelessly, and do what is right . . .

That doesn't mean we have to be perfect, to live without ever doing wrong. That's inhuman. It does mean we live in a way that focuses utterly on knowing and serving God.

2b [those who] speak the truth from their heart;

Be authentic. Be yourself. When you know and accept yourself as God's unique child, you will be honest in everything. Because it will come right out of your heart.

3 who do not slander with their tongue, and do no evil to their friends, nor take up a reproach against their neighbors;

How you treat your friends says a huge amount about the kind of person you are. What do you tell other people about them? Do you run them down or build them up? Love, serve, and honor all who are close to you, always.

4 in whose eyes the wicked are despised, but who honor those who fear the LORD; who stand by their oath even to their hurt;

Be known as one who can be trusted to do what you say. It may even hurt you to do what you promised, to be available to those who need you. It may cost you time, money, and lots of energy. But this way you and your words are always on the same page. That's integrity.

5a who do not lend money at interest, and do not take a bribe against the innocent.

Give freely with no strings attached. After all, your money and your resources are not really yours, are they? God gave them to you for a reason. Sure, you have to pay your bills and fulfill your obligations. But be generous and honest in all your dealings with others, especially those in need.

5b Those who do these things shall never be moved.

Is it that simple? Or rather, that difficult? There aren't very many to-dos here, but how naturally do they come to you? How well are you already doing these things? What do you need to focus on?

It's a lifelong project to work on these things. But you can abide with God in the process. As long as your heart is in the effort, as long as you desire to "walk blamelessly" with your God, you're there. It may not feel like it at times, and there will surely come times when you absolutely crash into the wall of selfishness. But even in those times, you're dwelling. You're abiding. You're present with God in the secret, holy, life-giving place.

And there, you cannot be moved. Or shoved. Or pushed out into the cold. Whatever grief comes your way, you will be in a place where you can get through it. And praise God in the end.

God, this is quite a project. But let me not see it as a bunch of to-dos or rights-and-wrongs. Let me see it as the natural outflow of being with you. Of living in your presence, under your challenging hand, in your loving arms. Right now and always. Let me know that I am truly abiding with you, dwelling with you, so that I can in turn share all that I gain from being in your presence with others in every part of my day.

Directed

Psalm 16

THEMES
Future
Life
Fulfillment
Purpose
Joy
Trust

1 Protect me, O God, for in you I take refuge.

Adolescence can be an exciting time of life. Your future is pretty much ahead of you. You hope it's a good one. You want a meaningful life, a good career, happiness, rewards. But you have to figure out how to move in the right direction—whatever that might be for you. And there's a lot going on in those turbulent years that you need to be protected from in order to make it to your future.

I'll confess it: I was a good kid, relatively. An innocent teenager—if there is such a thing. I was a PK—preacher's kid—and so my parents just expected me to behave. And I tried to, honestly. Oh, there were times we won't get into right now. But I really wanted to do something positive and constructive with my life. And I wanted to do it with God.

The psalmist can serve as an example for us on how to find our directions in this journey toward fulfillment. He begged for God's presence and protection in the process. And in this psalm he shows us how to walk the directed path of life in God's protective embrace.

2 I say to the LORD, "You are my Lord; I have no good apart from you." . . .

When you seek to live in the shielding refuge of God's presence, when you realize that life outside of God brings nothing good in the end, then you are on the right path. And wherever it takes you, up or down, backward or forward, down rabbit trails or speeding down expressways, if that is what you seek, you will ultimately find and experience peace and fulfillment.

7 I bless the LORD who gives me counsel; in the night also my heart instructs me.

To bless the Lord implies honoring God, submitting or surrendering to God. Trusting God when you can't see the path ahead, when you haven't a clue what's coming next. Blessing God opens the channel to receive God's wisdom, which may come in unexpected, surprising, and even very frustrating ways. Or not. When you bless God, you can listen to your heart. You can know that the inner impulses are real and true. You can discern the way ahead when the time is right. It may be dark. You may be tired and sleepless. But listen and you will hear. You will know what to do and where to go next.

8 I keep the LORD always before me; because he is at my right hand, I shall not be moved.

9 Therefore my heart is glad, and my soul rejoices; my body also rests secure. . . .

Be aware of God's presence always. Let your soul's default position be at God's right hand. And no matter what happens, no matter where the path of life takes you, you will be strong. You will sing for joy. You will know God's security. You will thrive.

And here is the end result of desiring to be with God through your life:

11 You show me the path of life. In your presence there is fullness of joy; in your right hand are pleasures forevermore.

In God's presence, you find direction in life that ultimately leads to joy and fulfillment.

When I was in high school, I memorized this verse because it captured what I wanted. Of course, in some ways I am thankful that God didn't actually show me in any detail way back then the exact path my life would take. Looking back now, if I had known then what I would face over the ensuing years—and all the fears and pains and struggles and reversals and confusions and losses and horrible mistakes—I probably would have run away from it.

But the psalmist isn't talking about God revealing a detailed plan for one's life. He isn't promising that God will reveal where life will take you, personally. He's talking about the God-directed and protected way of life that leads to fulfillment and purpose, that brings about fullness of joy, that results in pleasures forevermore, close beside God.

If you want it, that can be your way of life as well, starting right now, whatever your age may be.

God, I get so distracted. And fearful. I don't know what direction I'm going, or even which way I want to go. Help me get my home base settled: your presence. That's where I want to be. That's where I want to start. But that doesn't mean I want to get stuck there. I want to move. I want to live. I want to get out there and make life memorable. I want to feel your pleasure in whatever I do. I want to be creative even with life's mundane tasks. I want to know you're with me and I'm with you every step of the way. I want a rejoicing soul. I want an applauding God.

Distressed

Psalm 18

THEMES
Distress
Overwhelmed
Strength
Refuge
Protection

1 I love you, O LORD, my strength.

Can you remember the last time you said "I love you" to someone? Perhaps the words brought tears to your eyes as you expressed them, because you meant them down deep to your core. Or maybe they were just casually tossed off as you were leaving for the day.

The Hebrew word for "love" in this verse is powerful. The psalmist isn't just tossing out a "love ya, God!" The word he chose speaks of depth and fervor and passion. And what's interesting is that, according to this psalm's descriptive header, this was written during a deeply distressing time in his life.

Of course, when I find myself stressed out and overwhelmed by frustrations and fears, loving God passionately is pretty much the last thought on my mind. Rather than declaring my fervent love for God, I want to blame and threaten and moan. Instead of stepping back, rising above the situation and seeing the big picture that's already in God's strong hands, I focus on the pain and what's causing it.

The psalmist didn't do that. So it might help us when we find ourselves in stressful situations to run through in our hearts and minds the qualities of God's care, as the psalmist does:

2 The LORD is my rock, my fortress, and my deliverer, my God, my rock in whom I take refuge, my shield, and the horn of my salvation, my stronghold.

3 I call upon the LORD, who is worthy to be praised, so I shall be saved from my enemies.

Think about these descriptions—let them sink in deep. God is:

- *my rock*: strong, solid, immovable ground to stand on;
- *my fortress, my stronghold*: protecting me, providing all I need so that nothing and nobody can get to me;
- *my deliverer*: God can rescue me, carry me to safety and security;
- *my shield*: surrounding me, protecting me, defending me;
- *my salvation*: bringing me through it, making me whole;
- *my God*: intimately loved, trusted, known, surrendered to, and worthy to be praised.

24

And when you know that God is these things for you, you will be saved. Even when you feel like the psalmist did:

4 The cords of death encompassed me; the torrents of perdition assailed me;

5 the cords of Sheol entangled me; the snares of death confronted me.

You've felt that way too, haven't you? As though every possible negative thing had its scaly clawed fingers around your chest. You're all tied up by fear. Your emotions are in a wad, tangled up to the point you can hardly breathe. Whether it's some relationship crisis, financial reversal, job or school disaster—it has you firmly in its clutches. That is exactly the time to cry out to God for help.

6 In my distress I called upon the LORD; to my God I cried for help. From his temple he heard my voice, and my cry to him reached his ears.

Don't let yourself drown in your anxiety. Call on God. Remember who God is, and what God has promised you.

In fact, that's just how the psalmist started out with this psalm. He didn't start with his problem or his emotional condition. He started with his relationship with God, expressing his deep, unshakable love for his mighty God. He began by reminding himself, right in the midst of the chaos of his life, who the God he worships truly is.

When life has you in distress, when you are surrounded by fears and uncertainties, start with God. Express your love for God. Remind yourself who God is. And get through it to safety.

God, no matter what I face today, whatever the fear or crisis or need that has me so distressed and distracted, let me experience you as my rock, my fortress, my shield, my salvation, my God. Let me say—and mean—the words the psalmist wrote: "I love you, O Lord, my strength."

Messaged

Psalm 19

THEMES
Creation
Stewardship
Environment
World
Responsibility

Your e-mail in-boxes are full to overflowing. Your phone is vibrating with text messages. Instant messages, voice mails, phone calls, blog comments, hallway conversations—there is no end of the messages bouncing around us. Sometimes you can be getting so many that you're not paying any attention to any of them. But are you paying attention to those messages that are of utmost importance?

1 The heavens are telling the glory of God; and the firmament proclaims his handiwork. . . .

There is a vital message we often miss. It's not in words, but it's all around us. It's the language of creation that never ends, the unceasing voiceless communication of the world around us.

The created universe can't stop talking about God.

The world around you—the sky above and the land under your feet—points to the incredible God behind it all.

What are you hearing? Do you know who the heavens and earth are talking about? Do you know the creative power of the One who is behind it all?

The word "pours forth" day to day to day to day, and night to night to night to night. You can't read it, you can't hear the words, but the message goes out continually to the ends of infinity. And then it bounces back again, like an ocean wave. Wave after wave of glory.

That's one way God is communicating with you. It's a message of creativity, beauty, strength, love, and responsibility. It's a challenge to open your eyes and your mind and your heart to see your part in the creation. It may be an infinitesimally small part, but it's a vital part.

Do you hear? Are you getting the message?

But the unceasing speech of creation is only one way God communicates with you. There's another:

7 The law of the LORD is perfect, reviving the soul; the decrees of the LORD are sure, making wise the simple;

8 the precepts of the LORD are right, rejoicing the heart; the commandment of the LORD is clear, enlightening the eyes; . . .

There's a world of creativity, beauty, strength, love, and responsibility also within God's word. There you'll find food for your soul, wisdom for living, heartfelt joy, and clear enlightenment. It too is a message that lasts forever.

It may be difficult to see how the Bible can matter to you today. It's a book written so many centuries ago by so many different people, a book that seems so localized to a particular nomadic tribe in one small corner of the world, a book that often seems so out of date with its rules and regulations, a book that seems rife with unanswered questions. What in the world are we doing reading it today—let alone trying to make its insights relevant to our problems and situations in the twenty-first century?

That's a great question, and well worth wrestling with. For the rest of your life. Because the psalmist reveals a great truth: The word of God is

10 More to be desired . . . than gold, even much fine gold; sweeter also than honey, and drippings of the honeycomb. . . .

Are you reading it? Are you getting the message? Are you arguing with what you read, letting it soak into your consciousness, doubting it, asking God about it, finding the word of God in it for you today?

It's hard work, but it's rewarding and enriching work. Pursuing it opens you up to the spirit of truth, the message God is trying to get across to you. It's coming from within the pages of the Bible, and it's coming from all around you in the world you live in.

14 Let the words of my mouth and the meditation of my heart be acceptable to you, O LORD, my rock and my redeemer.

God, it's so easy for me not to see beyond the end of my nose. To fail to open my ears and eyes—as well as my heart, mind, and soul—to the message that you're communicating all around me, through creation and through the word. I really want to hear you. And not only hear you, but to respond responsibly to your loving message.

Devastated

THEMES

Forsaken

Forgotten

Alone

Lonely

Crisis

1 My God, my God, why have you forsaken me?
Why are you so far from helping me, from the words
of my groaning?

A few years ago, someone I know went through a year in hell. Within the space of mere months, his marriage was abruptly devastated, destroyed by the revelation of betrayal. His finances were decimated by the expenses of starting over. His grown son fell victim to drugs, causing upheaval in the newly broken family. And the company he worked for hovered near bankruptcy, unless a proposed merger went through—and even if it did, his job could be eliminated. Due to the overwhelming stress, he lost something like thirty pounds in only a couple of months.

He admitted to me that he recognized that a major cause of many of his problems was himself and his own behavior, but it felt like, even so, much of what was happening was far beyond his control. He dreaded the sound of his cell phone ringing—what new tragedy or trial awaited him? He would change the ringtone every few months because he got so tired of the same musical notes potentially bringing more bad news.

Where was God in all this?

2 O my God, I cry by day, but you do not answer; and by night,
but find no rest.

Somehow, the psalmist hunkered down and made his way through it, day by day. In fact, at times, he almost seemed happier than ever. Perhaps he began to realize that so much of what was happening was truly out of his hands, and in God's hands. Whatever would happen, would happen, he learned, and God would get him through it, providing the resources he needed when he needed them. Sometimes it didn't feel or look like that was the case, but deep down he knew it was.

Like the psalmist, he came to a new truth:

3 Yet you are holy, enthroned on the praises of Israel.

4 In you our ancestors trusted; they trusted, and you delivered them.

5 To you they cried, and were saved; in you they trusted, and were
not put to shame.

When life comes at us fast, how can we get into this same state of mind? How do we accept the hand that's dealt to us–whether we win, lose, or draw? How do we trust God to make it work out?

Jesus found himself in a situation none of us will ever face in our lives: He was hanging on a cross, dying. He felt the same overwhelming abandonment that we occasionally do. According to Mark's gospel (15:34) Jesus uttered the very words of the first verse of this psalm on the cross. He didn't understand where his loving God could be in this.

And yet he knew, deep down, that God was at work.

Can we look at that man on the cross, that man who lived and died to reveal the love of God for us, so we would be emboldened to love just as wholly and recklessly, and find hope in the midst of our abandonment, our aloneness, our emptiness?

God, there are times when I wonder if my faith in you is justified. When life gets really messy, and you don't seem to be awake or aware of what is happening to me, I wonder. Where are you? Why aren't you doing something? Or maybe you are there, even in the midst of it all. Maybe you are doing something astonishing, something I have no clue about at this point, something that on the other side of all this will make some semblance of sense. Or maybe not. Even so, to you I cry, and am saved.

Protected

THEMES
Needs
Restoration
Rest
Fear
Comfort
Protection
Care

1 The LORD is my shepherd, I shall not want.

2 He makes me lie down in green pastures; he leads me beside still waters;

Life is threatening. Whether they come from the news media, advertising, or our political leaders, messages of fear get a response. Raising the threat levels in our lives seems to work.

Will that flu virus grow out of control and decimate the population, including you? Will your financial future fall apart because the economy goes south as you watch helplessly? Will that big project you've been working on at the office crash and burn, causing you to get thrown out on the street? Are your car tires safe and strong enough to protect your family? Will you have enough time to study adequately for finals? Will the terrorists win? Will your wrinkles or bad breath or yellow teeth repel the one you were hoping to impress? And what's this about an asteroid that might hit the earth in a dozen years or so?

What are you afraid of? Think about it, and you'll realize that fear pervades your life. If only you could live somewhere safe and peaceful. If only you could rest in the fact that you have all the protection and provision you need. If only. . . .

3 he restores my soul. He leads me in right paths for his name's sake.

Picture the shepherd leading you to food and rest under his watchful, protective gaze. Enabling you to find refreshment and restoration of your soul. Guiding you into the way that leads to goodness and fulfillment and joy.

That is what God offers each of us who trusts in God. You can rest. You can know that you are cared for. You can be restored.

And as a result:

4 Even though I walk through the darkest valley, I fear no evil; for you are with me. . . .

No fear. No matter what you face in life, from the inconclusive medical test your doctor is concerned about to that funny sound in your car's transmission—no fear.

From your best friend's decision to go to a different school across the country to the crazed dictator's threats of attack from across the world—no fear.

Even in the darkest days, even in the face of death itself—no fear.

For your shepherding Lord is with you. You are in God's embrace. All the days of your life.

God, keep me in your loving gaze. Keep me in your protective arms. Keep me in the green and peaceful shade. Keep me aware that you know, and you care, all about me. I realize that you aren't promising to remove all those fearful threats from my life— sometimes I just have to walk through dark valleys. But even in the midst of those threats, I need not fear evil. For you are with me.

Soaked

THEMES

Water

Creation

Fear

Trust

Security

Safety

Serenity

1 The earth is the LORD's and all that is in it, the world, and those who live in it;

2 for he has founded it on the seas, and established it on the rivers. . . .

I love the water—lakes, seas, rivers, oceans, creeks. Like many, I experience peace and serenity, even security, in the presence of water. So many memories come to me.

The creek in Ritter Park: playing and exploring under a summer sun . . . riding a sled in the winter down the snow-covered hill and soaring too far over the lip of the creek and into the icy cold, ankle-deep water . . . going there one spring with my junior high earth science class on a field trip, when classmates dared a guy to gulp down a live crawdad he'd found in a shallow eddy—and he did.

The Ohio River: the northwestern border of my home state, West Virginia, and the lovely ribbon of commerce and activity along my hometown, Huntington, where on holidays my family would take our little runabout for some skiing and swimming.

The James River in Virginia: a wide, vast, murky waterway surrounded by history and mystery, where my family spent just about every summer on vacation when I was a kid.

The Atlantic Ocean, the Gulf of Mexico, the Pacific, the South China Sea—from thunderous waterfalls in the Brazilian countryside to a mirror-surfaced man-made lake in North Georgia—they are all part of the world of God's creation.

How can you not respond in praise for such sights?

7 Lift up your heads, O gates! and be lifted up, O ancient doors! that the King of glory may come in.

8 Who is the King of glory? The LORD, strong and mighty, the LORD, mighty in battle.

Water may speak of peace to me, but it also speaks of power. I am nothing in it.

One time when I was almost seven, my family vacationed on a Florida beach. I was playing in the waves not far from the shore when suddenly a rogue wave grabbed me and threw me all over the place under its smothering grasp. I felt like I was drowning, but suddenly I was slammed onto the hard sand and managed to pull myself out.

When I was a boy of nine, my family spent some vacation time on the Chesapeake Bay. My brothers and sister and I put on life jackets and floated in the water. Somehow I drifted far beyond the dock, and suddenly realized with terror that I was surrounded by jellyfish. I froze with fear. My big brother Greg realized my plight, jumped into a rowboat, oared his way quickly out to me, and managed to pull me into safety, though I was covered with stinging red welts.

With such powerfully terrifying experiences when I was young, it makes me wonder why I crave the water so much, why I feel so centered and peaceful and alive when I gaze on a body of water and walk by it and play in it.

I think it goes back to our origins, and to the fact that water speaks both of the power and the care of God in creation. God calls life out of the primordial seas and establishes and oversees it all. I am a part of all this; a tiny, infinitesimal part to be sure, but still a part. And all of it, the psalmist says, is the Lord's. The earth and all that is in it, all who live in it, the seas and the rivers—it's all God's.

Do you see yourself in the great cycle of life? Do you know the power and the peace of God? Do you realize the part you are playing in the creation song of God?

God, you made the waters of the earth and you made me. Give me a sense of my place in this creation, enable me to enjoy it, and empower me to care for it more thoughtfully and willingly. Soak me with the water of your cleansing, refreshing, powerful life.

Shamed

THEMES

Shame

Righteousness

Mercy

Attacks

Integrity

Honesty

1 To you, O LORD, I lift up my soul.

2 O my God, in you I trust; do not let me be put to shame; do not let my enemies exult over me.

3 Do not let those who wait for you be put to shame; let them be ashamed who are wantonly treacherous.

You've seen it happen in political campaigns. Some foolish mistake from the past, even the distant past, comes back to haunt a candidate. Maybe he tried to hide a DUI conviction or some youthful felony. Or she befriended someone who turned out to be rather notorious—through no fault of hers. A long-forgotten embarrassing website he created years ago gets discovered. Perhaps she never completed the degree she said she had, or he didn't serve in the military the way he'd proclaimed.

Some of these shameful things that come back to haunt them are minor embarrassments. Others are deeply personal situations. Some are very serious matters, but long forgotten and forgiven.

But whatever it is, their opponents grab onto such tidbits with ravenous glee. They broadcast scathing and humiliating television spots until everybody knows about this horrible reality. And sometimes, whether deservedly or not, such shameful embarrassments destroy the candidate's chances.

I've had my share of embarrassing revelations; maybe you have too. Everybody has closets whose skeletal contents might be revealed for the world to see.

The psalmist knew that. He put himself in King David's place, surrounded and inundated by troubles, his enemies lying in wait, just waiting for him to stumble, or to reveal some shameful truth. David depended on God to protect him from shame—because the people of God depended on him to defend them against their enemies too.

David doesn't confess to any shameful secrets here—though if you read the Old Testament you could probably find a few he could. He asks God to protect him. But he knew he had a responsibility to keep himself from being publicly shamed. And he explains how:

4 Make me to know your ways, O LORD; teach me your paths.

5 Lead me in your truth, and teach me, for you are the God of my salvation; for you I wait all day long.

6 Be mindful of your mercy, O LORD, and of your steadfast love, for they have been from of old.

7 Do not remember the sins of my youth or my transgressions; according to your steadfast love remember me, for your goodness' sake, O LORD! . . .

How do we keep ourselves from getting into such situations? We get to know God. We learn how to live and serve as God's own. We walk in absolute integrity and righteousness, open to the work of God within us and through us.

And we trust God's mercy and forgiveness for whatever humiliating things in our past still haunt us. Because when we do, the shame that grips us will lose its power.

Our shame may be a deep, dark, festering wound. It may be old and perhaps even forgotten, but it continues to affect how we live and act and feel about ourselves now. And when we let it boil over into our consciousness, it makes us even more susceptible to falling. Keeps us vulnerable to further hurts and poor choices and even greater shame. And leaves us open to attack.

David realized there is a way to prevent this downward spiral. It starts with lifting your soul to the Lord. Turning your heart to God's outstretched, forgiving arms. And moving forward with God on the path of righteousness.

20 O guard my life, and deliver me; do not let me be put to shame, for I take refuge in you.

21 May integrity and uprightness preserve me, for I wait for you.

Wait for God in honesty and authenticity, and you will be delivered.

It starts with lifting your soul and offering your life to God—shameful warts and all.

God, you know me. And in your loving mercy you have accepted me totally—including all the shameful things from my past. You have cleaned me up. And now I am doing my best to walk with you in honesty and integrity. Please help me. Lead me in the way I should go. Because the last thing I want to do is bring dishonor to you.

Vindicated

THEMES
Integrity
Honesty
Authenticity
Identity
Acceptance
Reality

1 Vindicate me, O LORD, for I have walked in my integrity, and I have trusted in the LORD without wavering.

In recent years there seems to have been a growing tide of literary fakers. Fantastic memoirs marked by the unbelievable experiences of ostensibly real people have been, time after time, revealed to be partly or largely embellished, exaggerated, or enhanced, if not total fictitious shams. You probably recognize some of the authors' names: James Frey, Laura Albert (writing as JT LeRoy), Tim Barrus (Nasdijjj), Misha Defonseca, Stephen Glass—the list goes on.

In one incident, "Margaret B. Jones" wrote a "memoir" entitled *Love and Consequences* revealing her experiences as a mixed race girl who grew up in foster care in horrific circumstances in south-central Los Angeles, ending up selling drugs for a street gang. Critics swooned, until—just as her author tour was about to begin—it was determined that the story was wholly fabricated by a white woman named Margaret Seltzer, who grew up in an affluent home and graduated from a prestigious prep school. The embarrassed publisher was forced to recall all copies of the book.[6]

In light of the huge advances these so-called memoirists receive, the mammoth publicity efforts involved, and the dreams of fame and fortune for all, it's always stunning to find out that so many editors, publishers, and book reviewers—let alone readers—have been taken for a ride once again.

The disconnect here between fantasy and reality is striking. In a culture that seems to prize authenticity and integrity and "being yourself" more than ever, there seems to be a backlash of deceit by many who want to seem much better—or much worse—than they really are. As author and scholar Daniel Mendelsohn put it: "This trend sheds alarming light on a cultural moment in which the meanings of suffering, identity and 'reality' itself seem to have become dangerously slippery."[7]

And before we get to feeling too smug, let's ask ourselves how honest we are on our resumes, or our Facebook and MySpace pages.

What's up here? Why are we so determined to shade our experiences, or even invent them? Are we just fooling others, or are we fooling ourselves as well?

The psalmist makes a case for being absolutely true and real before God. He asks God for vindication from attacks on his character, because he walks in integrity.

2 Prove me, O LORD, and try me; test my heart and mind.

3 For your steadfast love is before my eyes, and I walk in faithfulness to you. . . .

We can't hide our true selves from God anyway, so why try? In fact, the psalmist asks God to test him in heart and mind, because he is confident God will find integrity in every area of his life. And he will be vindicated.

It comes down to knowing ourselves as God made us. Accepting that reality. And living fully in it, aiming to be the best and fullest individual that we can be, in the power and wisdom of God.

If we have trouble with that, perhaps there's an area of our life, our identity, or our past experiences, that we'd rather not own. It's embarrassing. Or it makes us too different than—or too much like—everyone else. Or it's very painful.

The truth is, all of us are in that situation in one way or another. And burying those unwanted aspects of our identity or our past only keeps them festering in the dark. It's time to shine the light on everything we are. And accept ourselves fully.

11 But as for me, I walk in my integrity; redeem me, and be gracious to me.

You may never write a memoir, but think about ways that you shade the truth about yourself to others. Or ways you totally hide the reality of who you are. And then remember: God knows you. And God loves you nevertheless.

God, there are some things I don't like about myself. Some experiences in my past that are hurtful or embarrassing. Some things I wish desperately that I could change. But this is me. The good, the bad, the ugly, the funny, the sad, the unique. Yes, the unique. You made me just like I am. Let me live in that. And walk with you in the most transparent authenticity and honesty that I can in the strength of your Spirit.

Afraid

THEMES
Fear
Powerlessness
Strength
Courage
Confidence

1 The LORD is my light and my salvation; whom shall I fear? The LORD is the stronghold of my life; of whom shall I be afraid? . . .

Fear once kept me from having an honest conversation with someone who needed to be encouraged to stop a self-destructive habit. I didn't want him to be mad at me, or abandon our friendship, so I let it ride, pretending it wasn't really that serious. And of course it was that serious.

Fear has also kept me from making myself comfortable among people who are very different from me, and who need–so much more than I do–food to survive, clothing to keep warm. I would rather spend my free time doing something I enjoy, something entertaining or relaxing, rather than going to the urban assistance center and volunteering.

Fear has kept me, more than once I'm sure, from introducing myself to someone I just knew would be a good and positive person in my life. What if he or she rejected me? Or worse, made fun of me?

Fear kept me hostage in a job that I increasingly felt compromised my integrity. But what if I couldn't find another job to support myself, one I enjoyed?

As I look back, I realize with sadness the profound impact fear has had on my life in so many ways. In most of these cases, however, I eventually came to trust God and step out in faith and courage, and I didn't regret what happened next. What I do regret is letting my fear hold me captive for as long as it did.

What is fear doing to you? How is it affecting the career you really want to pursue? The people you'd love to meet? The ministry you'd like to engage in? The life you yearn to lead? How is fear strangling your hopes and dreams?

3 Though an army encamp against me, my heart shall not fear; though war rise up against me, yet I will be confident. . . .

When we are in relationship with the God who loves and cares about us utterly, when we are ordering our lives with integrity and openness to whatever God might send our way, there is nothing to fear–even in the face of overwhelming odds. Nothing.

But how do we develop that confidence?

8 *"Come," my heart says, "seek his face!" Your face, LORD, do I seek. . . .*

Is your heart urging you to seek the face of the Lord? To bask in the accepting but challenging presence of God? In the light of that awesome presence, the fears that are hindering and entangling you are revealed. And they shrink away in the heat of holy love.

14 **Wait for the LORD; be strong, and let your heart take courage; wait for the LORD!**

Imagine your life without fear. Imagine being empowered by the courage that comes from knowing and trusting God, in every aspect of your life.

If that was reality, what might you be doing differently today? Who would you reach out to? What holy task might you finally volunteer for? What risks would you take for God?

God, I do realize the power that unhealthy fear has on my behavior, my attitudes, my whole life. I realize I may be missing out on something major that you have for me because I don't have the courage you want to instill in me. I'm waiting for you, God. Shine the light of your wholeness, your energetic love, onto those dark, fearful areas in my heart. I can't wait to see where you take me next.

Carried

THEMES

Strength

Trust

Help

Protection

Blessing

⁹ *O save your people, and bless your heritage;*
be their shepherd, and carry them forever.

Some years ago I kept my then two-and-a-half-year-old grandson Tyler with me at my apartment just about every weekend for several months to help out his family. If you know kids, then you know how much time and attention a toddler requires, especially one with as much energy and creativity as my grandson. I was wiped out after those weekend visits! But gloriously so.

We had fun exploring the neighborhood, visiting the playgrounds in nearby parks. We'd watch kids' TV shows together and find fun (and sometimes even healthy) stuff to eat. We'd read storybooks together and even pretend to be characters in the books we'd read.

Through it all, I wanted to give Tyler a sense of security and comfort in the midst of all the turmoil of his young life. I yearned for him to experience joy and, especially, hope.

At night, of course, he didn't want to go to sleep. I made a bed for him on the floor of my bedroom out of folded-over bedspreads and blankets and an old sleeping bag. I'd get down on the floor with him and we'd pray and talk and remember the day we'd had together. One evening as we were going through this routine, Tyler said, "Bagah (that was his name for me), I wish I could be right here all the time."

Well, that blew my mind. Here he was in a makeshift bed on the floor. I hadn't done anything special for him, just carried him around, fed him, tried to help him enjoy his time away as best he could. Somehow, though, he felt safe and cared for. And I was grateful to be able to provide that.

In a way exponentially more than that, God desires to care for us, to enable us in our tumultuous lives to know security, joy, and hope.

The psalmist, in the midst of a time of difficulty and despair, prayed a fourfold prayer that assumes God will answer, because that's just the way God is. And these are four things to meditate on, rest in, and embrace for yourself:

- *Save your people*—When we get into trouble, or find ourselves in turmoil, pain, fear, or need, when we face a brick wall with something fierce right behind us, save us, God.

- *Bless your heritage*—When those who love you and follow you and belong to you are in need of hope, meaning, joy, well-being, or peace, bless us, God.

- *Be their shepherd*—When your children are lost or hungry, when we are threatened by danger, shepherd us, God.

- *Carry them forever*—When we are exhausted from the stresses and trials of life, when we have no idea which direction to go, when we are powerless to move forward, carry us in your strong arms forever, God.

In a very small way, that's what I wanted to offer my grandson. That's what we are asking of God. That's what God will provide. And when God does, we will sing with the psalmist:

> *7 The LORD is my strength and my shield; in him my heart trusts; so I am helped, and my heart exults, and with my song I give thanks to him.*

God, there are times, like right now, I want to wad myself up in my warm sleeping bag and let you whisper to me and tell me good things. Words of hope and joy and promise. Save me. Bless me. Shepherd me. Carry me. And I will sing your praises with joy forever.

Overwhelmed

Psalm 29

THEMES

God

Strength

Majesty

Awe

Power

¹ Ascribe to the LORD, O heavenly beings, ascribe to the LORD glory and strength.

² Ascribe to the LORD the glory of his name; worship the LORD in holy splendor. . . .

How would you feel if you were summoned to the Oval Office to meet the president of the United States? A bit overwhelmed? I can hardly imagine it. The authority and importance of the office, and the one who serves there, would certainly hold me in awe. Would I even be able to get a word out? After all, I get flustered when I approach a favorite author at a signing and tentatively hold out my copy of his book for an autograph!

So how am I supposed to relate to this image of the all-powerful God who is so far above and beyond anything we could possibly relate to?

God overwhelms me. God is so far beyond my comprehension, so totally unlike me, so powerful and wise and glorious, that I can't help but feel very, very insignificant.

The psalmist, too, was awestruck by the wonder and power of God. It's as if he gets breathless while telling us about the impossibly immense strength and authority God possesses, calling us to worship the One who so totally deserves it.

In an almost hypnotic description in verses 3–9, the psalmist can hardly come up with enough vibrant ways to describe the voice of God.

He says the voice of the Lord

- is powerful;
- is full of majesty;
- breaks the cedars;
- flashes forth flames of fire;
- shakes the wilderness;
- causes the oaks to whirl;
- strips the forest bare.

This is the word of God. Stand back! Bow down! Or get knocked down by this immeasurable force.

Frankly, that's overwhelming to contemplate. It's certainly difficult to relate to. How are we supposed to relate to this God?

The psalmist gives us a clue in the conclusion of this hymn of praise, and it gives me something to grab on to, to hope and pray for, to begin to realize in my own little existence:

11 May the LORD give strength to his people! May the LORD bless his people with peace!

Wow. God can give some of that strength to us. Somehow we can rise above our weakness into God's presence and, even amid the powerful whirlwind of God's voice, experience peace:

- peace in the midst of thundering mighty waters
- peace in the midst of flashing fire
- peace in the midst of earthquakes in the wilderness
- peace in the midst of the forest stripped bare

God may be far above and beyond me in every way imaginable. But God is right here too, present in strength and peace. Present with you and me.

"And in his temple all say, 'Glory!'" (v. 9).

God, I want to gain a better appreciation of your glory and strength. I want to worship you in all your holy splendor. I want, frankly, to be blown away by your voice. And at the same time, I want to know you intimately, as the God of peace who is present with me. The God whose peace I can share with others as liberally as you share with me.

Abandoned

Psalm 31

THEMES
Loneliness
Abandonment
Connections
Deliverance
Trust

1 In you, O LORD, I seek refuge; do not let me ever be put to shame; in your righteousness deliver me.

2 Incline your ear to me; rescue me speedily. Be a rock of refuge for me, a strong fortress to save me. . . .

5a Into your hand I commit my spirit; . . .

There are times in life when our days are filled with the choking fog of loneliness. Friends and family seem to have abandoned us, failing to answer their phones or respond to desperate e-mails, leaving us in an empty wad. Our loneliness in that moment connects itself to past times of isolation and abandonment, and only grows larger and more complex, more suffocating.

In such times, we just want to climb into God's lap of quiet safety and lie in the fetal position.

The truth is, we are connected to others in so many ways. We live surrounded by family and neighbors. We work or go to school with countless others. We connect online through communities and websites. And even so, at times we can still be lonely as hell.

The psalmist captured the emotion of this phenomenon dramatically:

9 Be gracious to me, O LORD, for I am in distress; my eye wastes away from grief, my soul and body also.

10 For my life is spent with sorrow, and my years with sighing; my strength fails because of my misery, and my bones waste away. . . .

12 I have passed out of mind like one who is dead; I have become like a broken vessel. . . .

These are feelings that I'm sure Dang Thuy Tram experienced. She was a doctor who volunteered at age twenty-four to work in a Viet Cong hospital during the height of the Vietnam War. In the midst of incredible fear and suffering, she managed to keep a diary where she poured out her feelings of love for her family and friends, from whom she was so desperately separated, as well as her experiences of the terrors of the war and the frustrations of her healing work in such difficult circumstances.

One morning in June 1970, as she walked with others down a jungle trail, she was shot and killed by an American soldier. Among her possessions they found her diary. Despite orders to destroy it, the soldier who found it kept it at the urging of his Vietnamese translator, and many years later it was published.

44

It's a tragic story marked by compassion, dignity, and loneliness. In fact, Dr. Tram's final diary entry reads: *"I am no longer a child. I have grown up. I have passed trials of peril, but somehow, at this moment, I yearn deeply for Mom's caring hand. Even the hand of a dear one or that of an acquaintance would be enough. Come to me, squeeze my hand, know my loneliness, and give me the love, the strength to prevail on the perilous road before me."*[8]

I can't possibly absorb the enormity of Thuy Tram's experience, but I can appreciate it. And the fact that she was able to move on and continue serving the next day—though with a tragic end—speaks volumes to me.

All I know in such times is to join with the psalmist and say, whether I fully believe it not:

14 But I trust in you, O LORD; I say, "You are my God."

15 My times are in your hand; deliver me from the hand of my enemies and persecutors.

16 Let your face shine upon your servant; save me in your steadfast love.

Whatever the cause of our loneliness, in whatever way we've been abandoned, we can voice our trust in God to get us through it. We don't know where our path will lead, to be honest, but we can know God is with us on that path.

God, give me the strength to say along with the psalmist, "Into your hand I commit my spirit." Help me to be strong and take courage as I wait for you in my dark place. Let the warmth and light of your love break through in your good time.

Forgiven

THEMES
Forgiveness
Confession
Honesty
Authenticity
Guilt

1 Happy are those whose transgression is forgiven, whose sin is covered.

2 Happy are those to whom the LORD imputes no iniquity, and in whose spirit there is no deceit.

3 While I kept silence, my body wasted away through my groaning all day long.

4 For day and night your hand was heavy upon me; my strength was dried up as by the heat of summer.

5 Then I acknowledged my sin to you, and I did not hide my iniquity; I said, "I will confess my transgressions to the LORD," and you forgave the guilt of my sin. . . .

On April 10, 1980, a man wearing a gorilla mask approached a car in a supermarket parking lot. In the car, Helen and Michael Farr were counting the change from their purchase. She laughed when she realized she had two pennies left.

Just as they were about to pull out, the masked man jerked the driver-side door open and demanded, "I want all of your money!" Michael reached for his wallet, but the man shot him in the chest. As Helen jumped out of the car and ran into the store for help, she heard a second gunshot.

Michael and Helen had been married for thirty-six years.

Not long after the shooting, police were pretty sure who had done it: a man named Steven Jenkins. But they never were able to get the evidence needed to nail him on the charge. Later, Jenkins was jailed for another crime—and bragged to several fellow inmates about getting away with the Farr murder. One of his accomplices finally came forward to tell authorities what had happened because his conscience had bothered him all these years. He hadn't been with Jenkins at the time of the shooting, but he knew what had happened.

So after working twenty-eight years on this "cold case," detectives finally were able to bring it to trial. Yet despite the new evidence, it still wasn't an open-and-shut case. Jenkins pled not guilty.

During the trial in the Franklin County, Ohio, Common Pleas Court, Helen Farr—now a tiny but strong woman of ninety-four and a cousin of mine on my mother's side—sat in the witness stand and calmly and clearly shared the story of her husband's murder. She'd never seen the assailant's face because of the mask, but she recognized his voice when he spoke in court. How? "Because I have lived with that voice for twenty-eight years."

After Helen's dramatic testimony, the man changed his plea and confessed to voluntary manslaughter.

In Judge David Fais' courtroom, after Jenkins entered his new plea, Helen looked at the man who had murdered her husband and said, "In my Christian spirit, he is forgiven. But Mr. Jenkins will have to go appear before a higher court, a higher judge than Judge Fais, and I hope in the meantime he asks forgiveness of the Lord."[9]

I can't imagine living life knowing that I had murdered someone—and bragged about it. How can you possibly live with yourself? Even so, there is some hope—the man finally confessed.

Some of the scariest people I've come across may not be murderers, but they, like him, don't seem to give their sins a second thought. They live a hidden life of deception and duplicity, effortlessly covering their tracks, without the slightest wince about how they may be hurting other people, let alone themselves.

God desires that we live openly, honestly, without a shred of deceit. Some people don't get that. And there have been times, I confess, that I have fallen into that category.

Like the psalmist, I want to live a life of integrity. I want a heart that is happy, a past that is forgiven, a life that is open, a conscience that is clean. To live otherwise is to live in misery and weakness and guilt. And what kind of life is that?

The psalmist concludes this song:

> [11] *Be glad in the LORD and rejoice, O righteous, and shout for joy, all you upright in heart.*

The righteous and the upright aren't perfect people. They're forgiven people. They are honest, authentic people who make their mistakes, problems, fears, and failures known to God and make things right with people they've wounded in the process, as best they can. They don't hide their iniquity; they confess it and they make the matter right. They are glad, and they shout for joy, because they are made clean.

God, search my heart for the unexposed dark areas that are festering there, and hurting not only those around me, but myself. I want to be transparent to you, and to all. I want to live without deceit. I want to be forgiven. And I want to be forgiving. I know that is a hard thing to do, but it's the only way to live connected with you.

Answered

Psalm 34

THEMES
Blessing
Praise
God
Deliverance
Fear
Community

An auto insurance company had a popular ad campaign about all the unexpected troubles people can experience. The commercials showed sudden and surprising ways cars get damaged or destroyed. The ads, encouraging us viewers to be prepared, declared a simple truth we can all identify with: "Life comes at you fast."

The commercials were funny. But not so much in real life.

Life does come at us fast. A serious illness gets uncovered in a routine physical. A relationship explodes over a simple miscommunication, or a major act of betrayal. A job, which you've spent years in, gets downsized in a field that now is dying or being outsourced. A child or sibling gets into a world of trouble.

In a world like this, Psalm 34 tells us to do something unusual:

1 I will bless the LORD at all times; his praise shall continually be in my mouth.

2 My soul makes its boast in the LORD; let the humble hear and be glad.

What, we're supposed to praise God "at all times"? "Continually"? Even in the midst of this biting sandstorm of difficulties? We're supposed to boast about what the Lord is doing in all this?

When I was a young man, I used to visit an elderly woman who had lost a leg to diabetes. She had already outlived several of her grown children, and of the thirteen she'd given birth to, only about half that many had survived to adulthood in the first place. Her husband, who by all accounts was a bit of a scoundrel, had also passed away years earlier. She lived very simply—because she had to—in a converted garage apartment in the house of one of her few surviving children. During the time I knew her, I don't remember her ever getting out of the house.

Whenever I visited, she would encourage me to read a psalm to her. One time I read Psalm 34, and she smiled as I read these first verses. "Oh yes, I believe that," she said nodding. I noticed, though, that the smile on her face was a bit forced, her jaw clenched, her face taut. Her life had been filled with tragedy, but it looked like she was going to force herself to bless God, no matter what.

I admired the determination, but I never quite got it. It can be mighty hard to praise God and boast in the Lord honestly when life seems to be conspiring against you.

But the psalmist goes beyond himself—and reveals a key to how we can bless the Lord no matter what:

> ³ *O magnify the Lord with me, and let us exalt his name together.*

"With me . . . together." See, we need each other to be able to bless the Lord and experience true gladness in whatever circumstances we find ourselves. We need to pray together in community, hold each other close, lift each other up, and praise God together. We need the support, encouragement, and challenge of brothers and sisters who care for us and for one another. To help us see more clearly in the darkness, to share one another's burden, to look beyond the circumstances and see the living, loving God.

When that happens, then we can praise God honestly and fully and gladly. When that happens, there's liberation:

> ⁴ *I sought the Lord, and he answered me, and delivered me from all*
> *my fears.*

It starts with seeking the Lord, together. That brings God's response. That brings deliverance.

I don't know about you, but when I'm covered up by life's difficulties, when I'm paralyzed by fear or overwhelmed by uncertainty, I tend to withdraw to myself. That's the worst place to be.

That's exactly the time when we need to reach out to our community of faith, our friends in the Spirit, for support. Then we can sing in praise together.

God, I want to trust you to get me through this situation I'm in—and the uncertainty, the fear, the paralysis. Help me learn to praise you "at all times . . . continually," along with my brothers and sisters. Together let us lift you up and trust you for deliverance. Even in the darkness, thank you for shining on me.

Loved

Psalm 36

THEMES

Love
Faithfulness
Praise
Refuge
Abundance

5 Your steadfast love, O LORD, extends to the heavens, your faithfulness to the clouds. . . .

When he was president Bill Clinton shared a story about a man named Steve, whom he had met while helping to prepare holiday meals at a community shelter in the District of Columbia. The kitchen served three thousand meals a day for the homeless and hungry, and trained people for jobs to help turn their lives around.

"As a young man, Steve had a scholarship for college and his future looked bright," Clinton explained in a radio address. "But he made some mistakes, and as a result, he's been homeless for much of his adult life. At Christmastime, he might go see his mother for a day—but if it was cold, you'd most likely find Steve spending Christmas under a bus shelter or beside a steam grate.

"But this year, Steve found the D.C. Central Kitchen—and discovered it's never too late to change. He's been in their training program for two months now, and already he's been offered a job. He's clean and off the streets. Best of all, his mother—who never gave up on her son—is so proud. She told him, 'Steve, you don't have to be a doctor or a lawyer. I just want to know that when I close my eyes, you'll be able to stand on your own two feet."[10]

President Clinton told that story a decade ago, and you have to wonder where Steve is now. Wherever he is, I bet his mother still hasn't given up on him.

You probably know of mothers and fathers who, no matter what their children have done, have never given up on them. Maybe you're one of those children.

But that unyielding, unstoppable, relentless parental love fades to nothingness in comparison with the love God has for you.

The psalmist helps us better understand our loving connection with God. He proclaims that God's character is marked by faithful, steadfast love. God's stubborn, unshakable love is everywhere you can possibly be. It never falters or weakens. It permeates everything. It fills creation.

7 How precious is your steadfast love, O God! All people may take refuge in the shadow of your wings.

Take a few moments and think about this steadfast love of God for you. Revel in it. Soak it up. Realize that all people–even you!–can experience protection and rest and security in the loving presence of God, like defenseless chicks huddled against the warm breast of a mother hen.

8 They feast on the abundance of your house, and you give them drink from the river of your delights.

9 For with you is the fountain of life; in your light we see light.

Let this reality echo in your mind and quicken your heart. Feast on all that God offers you, drink up the wine of God's overflowing provisions of love and care. Let it calm and refresh you like a living fountain. Let it blast through you like a fire hose. Let it light up your life and your world.

God provides everything you need to flourish, if you will accept it. Celebrate the steadfast faithfulness of God, the life-changing love that will never give up on you.

God, it is good to take my eyes off my circumstances and my overwhelming responsibilities and look instead to you and your provision for me. I know that. Let me live it for a change. I thank you for your never-ending love and faithfulness for me. Let me experience the fountain of your blessings, and live my life in a way that brings light and blessing to everyone around me. Let me share your never-give-up love with the world.

Committed

Psalm 37

THEMES

Commitment

Delight

Trust

Security

Fulfillment

Justice

Patience

It's a question frequently asked of couples that have survived many years together: What's the secret? How have you maintained such a vibrant relationship all these years–without murdering each other?

There are a variety of responses, but some very common themes. One couple says you have to talk to one another every day, look forward to seeing each other and sharing what's happened in your day. Another says you have to enjoy doing things together. One says the secret is to have an awful lot of patience. Another advises that if you have an argument, you have to kiss and make up before bed. One funny guy said the secret to a long marriage is to stay alive. That certainly helps.

One couple interviewed by a reporter identified seven secrets to their long-lasting union: having realistic expectations about the other person and the relationship, speaking directly and honestly about your concerns, being selfless, enjoying life as much as you can, respecting one another, having fun together, and above all, being committed to one another so there are no deal breakers.[11]

It occurs to me that those are pretty good goals to keep in mind in building our relationship with God.

How do we maintain a meaningful, healthy, vibrant connection with God? The psalmist gives us some guidance. Take some time to meditate on each of these aspects about becoming and staying connected with God.

3 Trust in the LORD, and do good; so you will live in the land, and enjoy security.

It starts with trust: Committing yourself to God, being confident that God is there and will be there. But the psalmist urges us to go beyond mere faith. We're supposed to "do good." That's active. The rest of the Bible explains what doing good involves–serving the poor, the lonely, the homeless, the hurting, the widows and orphans. Proclaiming grace, living love, seeking justice.

And what's the natural response of trusting God and doing good? You'll live in the land of God's promise. This is all about hope, hope that God will eventually sort everything out and all will be well. You'll be home forever. You'll experience joyful well-being. Maybe not right now, in this moment. But stay connected to God and, deep down, you will experience that security forever.

4 Take delight in the LORD, and he will give you the desires of your heart.

Now it gets fun. When you are committed to God, trusting and doing good, you can take delight in God. Experience the joy and grace that comes from following the will of God, living authentically and purposefully. Let yourself go in God's loving, living presence.

And what happens as a result? God gives you your deeply cherished desires. If one is fully connected with God, trusting in God, doing good, taking delight in God, what do you think his or her heart's desires would involve? If one's heart is beating for justice and peace, pulsing in concert with the Lord's, your deep-down wishes are hardly going to be fame and fortune. Being connected with God will radically alter your desires in life. But the heart's desires God gives are far more meaningful and delightful.

5 Commit your way to the LORD; trust in him, and he will act.

6 He will make your vindication shine like the light, and the justice of your cause like the noonday.

As in marriage or any relationship, commitment involves a decision of the mind, will, and heart, essentially all of who you are. In this case, you commit yourself to seek God, follow God, and live in connection with God. I love the way an old Hebrew English Interlinear Psalter defines the verb *commit*: "Roll upon Jehovah thy way." Can you picture that? Roll your whole life onto God. It's trusting, resting, lying on top of God—it's a very intimate, almost physical image. Be there. Stay there.

And when you live your life in such intimate, confident trust, God will act on your behalf. Just as the morning light shines into the damp darkness of night, God will make your righteousness shine in the world.

So what if you are reading all this about connecting with God and just not feeling it? What if it's making very little impact on the way you live your life? Maybe you need to reconsider how you relate to God. Maybe you've made the connection all about yourself, rather than about God's ways for you. Maybe the desires of your heart aren't really lining up with what's best for you. Think about it. And while you do, listen again to the psalmist:

7 Be still before the LORD, and wait patiently for him. . . .

God, it really is clear how you want me to live my life, what I'm supposed to know and trust and be about. I want a real connection with you. I want my life to line up with your hopes and dreams for me. I want to commit my way to you, be confident in you, and live a life of righteousness and justice. Shine that noonday light of discernment on my heart, let me examine it in your spirit, and strengthen my connection with you. I know I will only be delighted when that happens.

Measured

Psalm 39

THEMES
Life
Death
Meaning
Purpose
Fulfillment

Sometimes I can't believe how old I've gotten. How did that happen?

How could the president of the United States be born after I was?

How can I remember TV shows I watched four and five decades ago as if it were only yesterday?

How can people in the obituary column of the newspaper be so much younger than I am?

Life goes by so fast. It is so brief, and so fragile. My family has lost many members far too young. A cousin who was killed in Vietnam. An aunt who succumbed to cancer too early in life. A young nephew whose sudden death reverberates painfully years and years later. Why?

Life is frail and fleeting–maddeningly so. In fact, the psalmist demanded of God:

4 "LORD, let me know my end, and what is the measure of my days; let me know how fleeting my life is.

Frankly, I'm not sure I want to know my end, or how many days left I have. There are some morbid websites online where you can type in your birth date, answer some questions about your health and lifestyle, and they'll tell you exactly how many more days and hours you have left to live. Of course, they don't know, really–it's just based on insurance charts and mortality averages. Even so, I don't want to know.

5 You have made my days a few handbreadths, and my lifetime is as nothing in your sight. Surely everyone stands as a mere breath. . . .

The psalmist realizes that in the grand scheme of things, one's life is short. A mere breath. A nothing.

I don't want to know how many more breaths I have left to take. But I do want to treasure whatever time I do have left. I do want to make that time as meaningful and life-giving and joyful as I can. I want the "few handbreadths" of my days to matter.

How do we do that? We value every moment God gives us, intentionally appreciating what a gift it is. We keep in mind that life is short and time's a-wasting—not just to keep busy and become exhausted by activity, as that only hastens our last hour. But to live purposefully, with goals to accomplish and dreams to fulfill. To live creatively. Lovingly. Living to the full. Reaching out. Risking. Squeezing the best out of the life God has given us.

We live, in short, in such a way that those who know and love us, those we've known and loved and served, will always remember us—not sorrowfully, not filled with grief over losing us, but filled with inspiration, marveling how utterly and fully and richly we lived our lives in the measureless grace of God.

7 And now, O LORD, what do I wait for? My hope is in you.

God, rather than sitting and waiting and wasting the precious time I have on this earth, let me spend it wisely and fully. Help me make this life you've given me in turn a gift to you and to others. Give me the sense to appreciate, to revel in, my days. And to love and serve you as fully and wholly as I can, day by day, until the end. Which, thankfully, is only the beginning with you.

Conflicted

Psalm 41

THEMES

Poverty

Blessing

Happiness

Help

Volunteering

Ministry

Homelessness

1 Happy are those who consider the poor; the LORD delivers them in the day of trouble.

2 The LORD protects them and keeps them alive; they are called happy in the land. You do not give them up to the will of their enemies.

I work in midtown Atlanta, an urban area where numerous homeless people walk the streets. When I first started working in the area I kept a couple of dollar bills in my pocket, and anytime someone stopped me asking for money I'd hand it over. But then I heard people who work with the homeless advising not to do that, because rarely was the money used for the purpose for which it was asked, but rather for drink or drugs. So I started suggesting to those who approached me for money that they go to a nearby center operated by several churches where they could get the food and housing assistance they needed. Often, that suggestion was met by a shrug, or worse.

I really don't know how to help the poor. There are numerous ministries and service agencies where I could volunteer or contribute to, and maybe I will again someday when I have the time. In the meantime, it's frustrating, and a little scary, to be approached by someone so dirty and unkempt and needy. So different.

As difficult as it can be in Atlanta, it was worse when I visited Rio de Janeiro. In the evenings and nights, the wide sidewalks in Ipanema fronting upscale shops and stores were often crowded with homeless people, even children and families. Some were in obvious physical distress having lost feet or whole limbs.

Children were often sent from the favelas to beg for money in whatever ways they could. One morning in Rio I was looking out the window of my hotel restaurant, where I was enjoying an abundant breakfast buffet, and saw a girl of perhaps eight sitting on the curb of the street. When the traffic light turned red, she would hop out in the middle of the street and juggle three worn tennis balls, just for a few seconds, and then move to the driver's window with a pitiful, serious look on her face. Sometimes the window would go down and a Brazilian real or two would be passed into her little hand. More often, though, the window stayed up, the driver studiously avoided looking at the girl's face until the light turned green, and she was left standing in the exhaust fumes. She worked at this for the half hour I sat in the restaurant, watching her. It broke my heart. Did she do this every day?

Jesus said the poor will always be with us (Matt. 26:11). Nevertheless, time and time again the Bible urges us to make helping the poor, the weak, the helpless a high priority of our lives.

The psalmist tells us that those who keep the poor and the weak on their mind and in their hearts are "happy." God will look after them and provide for them, protect them from harm. They will be rewarded.

That doesn't mean we should serve in order to feel good. But it should force us to wrestle with what all this means to us personally. How will we consider the poor and weak? How much can we give? To what organizations or ministries? Where can we volunteer at a soup kitchen, or stay overnight at a shelter? In other words, how can we do our part to minister the healing love of God for those who are hurting the most?

God honors those who make it a priority in life to wrestle with these questions—and to do something about answering them. Doing so puts our own lives into deep perspective, so that whatever our circumstances, we can realize how happy we truly are.

God, I confess I so often turn my eyes from the need that stands right in front of me. Contributing to ministries that serve the poor is so far down my list of financial priorities that I'm embarrassed. Let alone actually volunteering in some way at my church or community organization. I want to "consider the poor." I want to figure out how I can be best involved in doing what I can to help those who are on your heart. Help me to grapple with this today. Not just to make myself happy, but them. And you.

Parched

THEMES
Anxiety
Abandonment
Loneliness
Hope
Thirst

¹ As a deer longs for flowing streams, so my soul longs for you, O God.

² My soul thirsts for God, for the living God. When shall I come and behold the face of God?

Instinct is a powerful mechanism in the animal kingdom. Instinct enables species to survive and thrive by guiding them in certain mysterious ways even from birth. I'm always amazed to watch documentaries, for instance, that show sea turtles traveling hundreds or even thousands of miles to return to the particular beach from which they hatched in order to lay their eggs—and then witness those hatchlings instinctively heading to the sea to start the cycle all over again.

Salmon defy all odds against a raging river current to return to their spawning grounds. Spiders practice the intricate art of web making in order to get the food they need to survive. Countless species follow precise innate behaviors to protect themselves from predators on the one hand and to lure their next meal on the other.

The examples are endless and fascinating. But if for some reason an animal ignores instinctual behavior, it is not long for this world.

When it comes to seeking God's presence, I feel an instinctual yearning. It's a holy lust. A spiritually magnetic pull. A longing so deep in my soul that it feels as powerful as the tides of the earth.

Whether I am giddy at a sudden positive turn of life, fretful about the future, or despondent about a loss, whatever the circumstance I want to be in God's presence to share it, reflect with God on it, praise God, or seek God's comfort.

And if anything hinders that longing—whether my circumstances, my choices, my laziness, my distractions—then truly I will not survive, and cannot thrive.

The psalmist felt it, comparing himself to the thirsty deer, yearning for refreshment in the presence of the Creator. That thirst demands to be quenched. And it can be quenched in healthy ways or unhealthy ways.

The world offers innumerable ways to deal with our innate thirst for God's presence. And you know how easy it is to pursue them. We deaden ourselves to this inborn drive or try to fill it with spiritual junk food. We fill our days with the all the distractions of the media or sex or empty success. And unless we surrender to the pull of God's presence, we will not survive.

If we're not sensing the refreshing presence of God, the fault is likely not God's. The psalmist recognized this at a time when he felt abandoned by God, alone in his thirst.

3 My tears have been my food day and night, while people say to me continually, "Where is your God?"

4 These things I remember, as I pour out my soul: how I went with the throng, and led them in procession to the house of God, with glad shouts and songs of thanksgiving, a multitude keeping festival. . . .

He remembered what it was like when his longing was satisfied and his thirst quenched. The joyful company of his fellow worshipers surrounded him then. He wanted to get back to that place. He wanted to be with God once again, and always.

It's amazing how present and lively God can be for you when you let God have all of you—when you let all of who you are be known and loved. Sure, I've experienced countless times of feeling alone and abandoned, when the tears of loss and fear would run off my chin. But those are times that come and go. Paradoxically, the deep sense of alienation is dissipated only when we let our longing for God grow. Because that's when God fulfills it.

If your soul is resonating with this sense of alienation and abandonment, you are no doubt asking yourself what the psalmist asked so many years ago, and what I have asked of myself from time to time in this life:

11 Why are you cast down, O my soul, and why are you disquieted within me? Hope in God; for I shall again praise him, my help and my God.

Why indeed? Hope in God. Let yourself long for God's embracing presence. It's not that hard. We really don't have to work at it. We simply need to follow our spiritual instinct as God's created and beloved child. And let the restoring waters of the Spirit flow.

God, I am thirsty. It's a thirst that I know can't be quenched by any drink. There are no quick fixes. It's a soul-deep longing for you. If there's something within me that's hindering the flow of your Spirit—some dishonesty, something lacking, some denial of reality, some fear, some distraction—let me own it, and give it to you. I'm ready for your Spirit to flow through me, and I want to be a channel of your flowing peace and love to others.

Changed

THEMES
Change
Disaster
Fear
Safety
Protection
Quiet

1 God is our refuge and strength, a very present help in trouble.

2 Therefore we will not fear, though the earth should change, though the mountains shake in the heart of the sea;

3 though its waters roar and foam, though the mountains tremble with its tumult. . . .

Every once in a while you'll see a story in the news about someone who fell into a coma years ago, and then one day suddenly woke up. In one case a year or so ago, a Polish railway worker who'd been hit by a train had been unconscious for nineteen years. Nineteen years! Until one day he woke up and started talking. He soon discovered his country was no longer under Communist rule, food was no longer scarce, and an array of amazing things had happened in those nineteen years. "Now I see people on the streets with mobile phones and there are so many goods in the shops it makes my head spin," he said in a television report.[12]

I've often wondered how such Rip Van Winkles cope upon waking up. It's hard enough to keep up with all the tumultuous change in our world—much of which can be terrifying. Wars, attacks, natural disasters, street fighting, political rises and falls, on and on the changes come.

One of the first things I do in the morning after I pour my cup of coffee is to go online and, before I even check my e-mail, I click on the latest news headlines. Truly, my heart races a bit: What has happened during the night to change the world we live in, for good or for bad? Usually I find a little solace in learning that nothing major blew up. But what do we do when we're confronted by earthshaking change? Where can we go for safety?

5 God is in the midst of the city; it shall not be moved; God will help it when the morning dawns.

6 The nations are in an uproar, the kingdoms totter; he utters his voice, the earth melts. . . .

We may not understand what's going on. We may have no idea what's coming next. But we can turn to our loving, all-powerful God in faith. No matter what changes shatter the status quo of the world, God is here in our midst. And God is immovable, unchangeable, and ready and able to help.

Sometimes in the midst of the tumult, overwhelmed by the change, we forget that. God's voice breaks through the noise and speaks clearly to us:

10 *"Be still, and know that I am God! I am exalted among the nations, I am exalted in the earth."*

The "be still" is comforting. The Hebrew word has the sense that God is saying, "Enough! Stop it! Be quiet!" As though we are kids running around, screaming, trying to find a place to hide.

Stop. Be quiet. Be still. Find your place of refuge with me, God says, and we'll get through this just fine. It may be scary. It may even hurt. But, after all, I am God.

God, sometimes it feels as though I'm racing in directions I have no idea where I'm heading, and my tachometer is over the redline. Change assaults me day by day. Not only in my own life, but also in the world. Every moment brings something unexpected. Without you to anchor me, to strengthen and protect me, I would be overwhelmed. Thank you for being the exalted God who knows and acts and is. Thank you that in the midst of a world of change, you are the changeless One.

Overjoyed

THEMES
Celebration
Praise
Joy
Thankfulness
Victory

1 Clap your hands, all you peoples; shout to God with loud songs of joy.

2 For the LORD, the Most High, is awesome, a great king over all the earth.

Together again for Thanksgiving, my brothers and sister and I decided to watch a DVD together: *We Are Marshall,* based on the true story of the 1970 plane crash that killed nearly every member of the Marshall University football team, as well as numerous pillars of Huntington, West Virginia, business and society. We'd all seen the movie before, but we wanted to watch it together—because each of us is a Marshall graduate and had lived through the tragedy that changed the school and the city forever. In fact, as a high school student on a class trip to Washington, D.C., I happened to be on the last airliner that left Huntington's Tri-State airport before the fated Marshall plane attempted to land in a storm and missed the runway.

As my siblings and I watched, we pointed out locations familiar to us—our campus, the downtown movie theater, a local cemetery—and complained about some of the acting. Even so, the story was still moving, because we knew it well. The university president tried persistently to find a coach willing to rebuild the program on the ashes of disaster, until Jack Lengyel finally rose to the occasion. It was almost impossible to create a team around the very few players who had not made the flight to play East Carolina because of injury or disciplinary reasons. Yet they worked tirelessly to make it happen despite the lack of potential players and rules that prevented freshmen from playing. The odds were overwhelming. The school came close to pulling the plug on the whole program.

But, as the movie revealed, it all came together and the next season Marshall—against impossible odds—won its home opener against Xavier University in an emotional and dramatic victory. As you can imagine, the home crowd went wild with a cathartic celebration, and as we watched it again, it was still impossible to keep the tears from welling up.

Of course, Marshall got blown out by their next opponent. In fact, they didn't have a winning season for another dozen years or more. But that initial celebration fueled a resurgence in the school and community that healed wounds and brought people together.

There are plenty of causes for celebration in the world—from winning football games to political campaigns, from landing a promotion to capturing someone's heart. Yet they all fade away to nothingness when you consider the celebration you can get in on right now: the celestial celebration that spans generations, worlds, and dimensions—the ecstatic worship of our awesome God.

5 God has gone up with a shout, the LORD with the sound of a trumpet.

6 Sing praises to God, sing praises; sing praises to our King, sing praises.

7 For God is the king of all the earth; sing praises with a psalm.

All peoples of the world are invited to join the party. Yes, all peoples. And don't be quiet about it. Clap loudly. Shout. Sing songs of joy as uproariously and lustily as you can. God deserves our energetic praise far more than our favorite sports teams.

Maybe you feel you haven't received your Evite to this party yet. Maybe you consider it just a little silly, with all the fear and frustration and emptiness you're feeling right now. Or you're overwhelmed by the long road ahead of you and the seeming impossibility of arriving somewhere. Understandable.

But I wonder what would happen if you celebrated a little by faith.

What if you started thinking about all the things you're thankful to God for?

What if you let yourself know, deep down, that you are one whom God loves?

What if you started singing a song of praise and clapping your hands, just a little bit?

It might feel rather silly at first. But who knows, you might get into it. You might realize the truth behind it. You might get the hope you need to keep moving forward despite the odds. You might just find yourself right in the midst of the everlasting celebration.

God, I think I hear some of that happy noise, deep down inside me. Let it come out in praise and joyful celebration. I have so much to be thankful for. You have given me so much. A little singing and praising is the least I could do to thank you for your awesomeness.

Possessed

Psalm 49

THEMES
Wealth
Possessions
Meaning
Envy
Poverty

5 Why should I fear in times of trouble, when the iniquity of my persecutors surrounds me,

6 those who trust in their wealth and boast of the abundance of their riches?

This morning I read that somebody in Ohio just won $207 million in the latest Mega Millions lottery. I wonder what will happen to him or her.

Sometimes I read about those who had that dream come true, who were consumed by the sheer joy of winning, only to find that having to manage the resulting life and all its responsibilities and challenges requires far more discipline and knowledge than they ever had. Some of them simply self-destruct in an orgy of spending and living the "good life."

Some years ago a church-going man won a huge lottery jackpot and ended up totally possessed by his newfound possessions and in horrendous legal trouble, having squandered most of it on all sorts of sordid activities—after giving a nice chunk, of course, to his church. Before long, his health and his piggy bank were both broken.

Of course, I tell myself, I would handle such a windfall with the utmost wisdom and grace. I have a checklist: I would enable my family members to live comfortably but, let's be reasonable, not outrageously. I would certainly give a substantial chunk to my church and the organization I work for, perhaps some other worthy ministries, and maybe I'd even set up a foundation. But I would also enjoy life, perhaps do a good bit of traveling, visiting my homes in the mountains and on the beach and perhaps a simple place somewhere in Europe. . . . And what sorts of cars would I drive? And . . .

Then I wake up, and I move on with reality. Which, despite the fact that I am hardly wealthy, is not so bad. And as I do, I hope I keep the message of this psalm in mind.

7 Truly, no ransom avails for one's life, there is no price one can give to God for it.

8 For the ransom of life is costly, and can never suffice,

9 that one should live on forever and never see the grave.

10 When we look at the wise, they die; fool and dolt perish together and leave their wealth to others.

11 Their graves are their homes forever, their dwelling places to all generations, though they named lands their own. . . .

We cannot buy fulfillment, we cannot pay our way into heaven. Wealth cannot keep us from dying—though it might put death off a bit or make us look a little younger, having had some work done, before it happens to us.

All right, yes, we know this. Money doesn't buy happiness. But it can be a comforting thought. Sure, some people have wealth foisted on them suddenly, others are born into it, and still others work their fingers to the bone to make it. We, however, can congratulate ourselves for not being part of their number, or at least for not letting what wealth we do have distract us from what's important in life, right? We can sing with the psalmist:

15 But God will ransom my soul from the power of Sheol, for he will receive me.

And yet, my personal battle is not so much about wishing I had more money than I know what to do with. It's about envying those who do.

It's easy to make excuses about our life when we are paying attention to the financial resources others have to live theirs. We can get so eaten up by jealousy over all the gadgets, cars, houses, and trinkets others have that we ignore all the priceless blessings we do have.

Let's not get sidetracked from our own work and calling and holy interests by being envious of others. Let's keep the bigger picture in mind:

16 Do not be afraid when some become rich, when the wealth of their houses increases.

17 For when they die they will carry nothing away; their wealth will not go down after them.

18 Though in their lifetime they count themselves happy—for you are praised when you do well for yourself—

19 they will go to the company of their ancestors, who will never again see the light.

Just like the rest of us, wealthy human beings are mortal. Though they may have "happy lives" now with lots of fame as successful people with hardly a care, they will end up the same way we all do. Dead. And whether they lose their wealth before or after they die, they still lose it.

God has provided everything we need for our souls to live forever in God's presence. God has made the way for us, ransoming our souls, to be received into God's presence forever. How much would you pay for that?

God, whatever life may bring my way, let me not hoard it in clenched fists, but open my hands to share and to give. Give me the strength to live the life you've given me to live, to strive to fulfill my calling as your unique creation, and to keep in mind the unsurpassable value—the absolute pricelessness—of my relationship with you.

Summoned

THEMES
God
Authority
Power
Sovereignty
Order
Creation

1 The mighty one, God the LORD, speaks and summons the earth from the rising of the sun to its setting.

Watching the sunrise can be an energizing experience. One of my favorite places to do that is St. Simons Island on the coast of Georgia. I started a practice some years ago of driving the six hours there from Atlanta, usually during Lent, to do some painting or writing, or just to get away and watch the sunrise and read and breathe deeply, just myself and God.

If I got up early enough, I would walk or run on the beach cleaned by the night's tide change. The few others who also do this generally have iPod earbuds plugged into their heads. For me, now is not the time for that. It's time to listen and to watch the seagulls, to see the tiny sand crabs scurry and dig in, to watch folks run their dogs, to gaze on the shrimp boats in the distance still harvesting the ocean, and to just be.

And seeing the one-and-only sunrise for that day, whether in a clear sky or one mottled by orange and pink clouds—that is worth it all.

A few years ago, I had a week's vacation on Key West, the end-of-the-line coral atoll in the Gulf of Mexico, where Hemingway and countless other authors and creative types found inspiration. Wherever you were on the island, as sunset approached, you'd make your way to Mallory Square to watch the show and perhaps toast the creative handiwork. When I went the square was packed with people of all ages and backgrounds, both locals and tourists. Numerous jugglers, actors, artists, comedians, singers, performers, and salespeople of all kinds worked the crowd. It was a noisy, multicultural celebration as we all watched the Gulf waters swallow the red-hot sun, eliciting a round of enthusiastic applause—quite the contrast from my quiet sunrise beach walks only a few hundred miles away on St. Simons Island.

One of those Mallory Square performers, a high-wire artist and juggler who has seen the sunset celebrations grow from a few dozen in 1976 to the several thousands that congregate today, had an insightful comment about the phenomenon: "It's more than a party—it's a sacrament," he said. "It revives the old practice of assembling in the town square to share important communal events."[13]

Think about some of the sunrises and sunsets you've experienced. What did you see and smell and hear? How did you feel? Weren't they marvelous and beautiful? Weren't they full of hope and a sense of well-being, that all is right with the world—that we've made it through yet another cycle?

Think about it, and then remember—and worship:

2 Out of Zion, the perfection of beauty, God shines forth.

Consider each new sunrise as a time when God summons you to enter the new day. God calls you to wake up and get about the business of living and loving and serving as creatively as God does.

That makes each sunrise an occasion to praise God for the new day, to applaud God's handiwork, and to pray for the wisdom and strength to make it the most amazing day possible. Then you can rest in God contentedly after sunset, and prepare for the next sunrise. And the next celebration.

God, shine on me today. Whether I actually see the sunrise or sunset today or not, keep me aware that you are in control, that you are over all creation. The world may be chaotic around me, but you are above all. You speak, you summon me, and I answer. Today. Tomorrow. Always. I yearn for this day to be all it possibly can be, full and beautiful and meaningful. So that when the sun sets, I can praise you for every moment. And anticipate the next sunrise with joy.

Cleansed

THEMES

Honesty

Humility

Forgiveness

Authenticity

Confession

1 Have mercy on me, O God, according to your steadfast love; according to your abundant mercy blot out my transgressions.

2 Wash me thoroughly from my iniquity, and cleanse me from my sin.

3 For I know my transgressions, and my sin is ever before me.

4 Against you, you alone, have I sinned, and done what is evil in your sight, so that you are justified in your sentence and blameless when you pass judgment. . . .

God considered King David of Israel to be "a man after my heart, who will carry out all my wishes" (Acts 13:22). That encourages me when I read Old Testament accounts about David's incredible lust, selfishness, fear, and occasional sheer stupidity. Because I can identify.

Sure, I want to be a person after God's heart. I want to live in the tidal wave of God's loving will. But I'll be the first to admit I can screw it up.

The psalmist had one of David's notorious experiences in mind when he considered God's mercy (2 Sam. 11–12). While taking an afternoon nap on the roof of his royal palace, the story goes, David saw a beautiful woman bathing in the courtyard of another building across the way. Suddenly, he had to have her. And though they were married to other people, he did have her. After a thwarted attempt to cover up his impregnating her, David even ultimately conspired to have her husband killed in battle to get him out of the way. It all sounds like a bad soap opera. Obviously, "the thing that David had done displeased the Lord" (2 Sam. 11:27b).

Nathan, a holy prophet, knew what the king had done. So he went to David and told him a story about a sweet little ewe lamb, the beloved pet of a poor man, which was taken by a ruthless rich man and cooked up for some company. David was furious with the rich man in that story. And he must have been shocked out of his sandals when Nathan charged, "You are the man!" In light of all he had done, David was far worse than the rich man of Nathan's little story.

David faced a turning point here. He could easily have reacted in anger and defensiveness. He could have tried to explain "his side of the story." As king he could have expelled Nathan from the kingdom or imprisoned him forever, even put him to death, in order to protect his reputation.

In other words, David could have gone to the dark side.

But David immediately responded out of a tender, honest heart. He realized how he had made a mess of things out of his poor choices and his selfish will. So he confessed and begged for God's mercy. And the psalmist attempted to capture the emotion of his heartfelt confession.

We all need to be cleansed from something. Perhaps it's a relationship that's unhealthy, or one we're misusing or even abusing. Maybe it's forcing some figures at work to make our balance sheet look better, or overbilling some customers. Maybe it's cheating on our coursework in school. Whether it's a stupid mistake that we're not willing to own or the result of our total rebellion from God's ways, there's some area of life that we know we have let get out of control, and we're getting to the point not of fixing it but of covering it up.

This is the time to learn from David's humble, honest response—before it's too late. This is the time to turn to God for cleansing.

Of course, though David was forgiven and cleansed by God, he still suffered the ramifications of his choices, including the death of the son that resulted from his affair. This is harsh. It's hard to take in at times. But if we're honest, each of us knows what it's like.

God has high standards. God wants us to be honest and true to ourselves, to each other, and to God. God hopes for us that we will be positive and giving and loving, not selfish and hurtful and deceptive. That's not always easy, and it certainly isn't as easy as messing up in the first place.

We need to keep connected to God's goals for us. We need to acknowledge that we don't have to do it all in our own power. God has given us everything we need to live this way. It starts by asking God, as David did, to:

10 *Create in me a clean heart, O God, and put a new and right spirit within me.*

11 *Do not cast me away from your presence, and do not take your holy spirit from me.*

12 *Restore to me the joy of your salvation, and sustain in me a willing spirit.*

13 *Then I will teach transgressors your ways, and sinners will return to you.*

God can renew and refurbish your spirit, your heart, your drive, your attitudes. God can give you a positive, willing, and steadfast spirit to live and learn from mistakes and change direction. Yes, God can. But it starts with the humble, honest response of your heart.

God, if I've been trying to fool you, or others, or even myself, shake me up with the truth. Open my eyes and my heart so I can be utterly honest. I beg for your cleansing restoration, for a willing spirit to pursue you, for a desire to tell others about what you've done for me and for them, and to show them how much you love them, no matter what. Thank you for the joy of a clean, open, renewed heart.

Rooted

Psalm 52

THEMES
Love
Steadfastness
Strength
Trust
Choices
Crises

One early spring night I was on my couch watching an old movie, noticing flashing lightning out the windows but not thinking much about it, when suddenly a warning siren began wailing at the fire station across the street. But before I could even worry about what was happening, let alone find cover, the storm had passed through my area of town and the siren was silenced. Just some heavy rain, nothing too serious.

It wasn't until the next morning that I learned to my shock that a tornado had struck downtown Atlanta, Georgia, the night before—mere blocks from where I live. Cars were crushed, hotel windows were blown out, the fabric roof of the Georgia Dome stadium was ripped to shreds in places, the CNN Center lost part of its roof, and a building collapsed. The whole central city was shut down for the emergency. I was astonished as I looked online at photos of the aftermath of this powerful windstorm.

What's surprising often in such cases is what is left standing after a storm like that. Structures you assumed were solid and immovable are reduced to rubble, while a sapling nearby stands strong. When the tornado winds of life buffet and assault us, as they no doubt do from time to time, what will keep us standing?

In Psalm 52 we read of the terrible storms that can overtake those who are evil:

> *5 But God will break you down forever; he will snatch and tear you from your tent; he will uproot you from the land of the living.*
>
> *6 The righteous will see, and fear, and will laugh at the evildoer, saying,*
>
> *7 "See the one who would not take refuge in God, but trusted in abundant riches, and sought refuge in wealth!"*

A rather terrifying fate—all the things such selfish people grasped onto for comfort and security are snatched away by a storm of judgment. Their money, possessions, even the luxurious tent they lived in—all the wealth they trusted and sought protection in—are all gone with the wind.

So what should we be trusting in?

> *8 But I am like a green olive tree in the house of God. I trust in the steadfast love of God forever and ever.*

In the Middle East, olive trees have deep, wide root systems because they work hard to seek whatever water they can find. As a result, olive trees are green; in fact, they are evergreen. They stay alive and fresh and strong. They are immovable. And if we can dig our roots deep down into the "steadfast love of God forever and ever," trusting in God no matter what the winds of life bring our way, we too can stand strong and immovable.

Bishop Gene Robinson, no stranger to the storms of life, writes of a weather satellite photo he saw at a crucial and stormy point in his life. It was taken far above a hurricane in the Atlantic: "In the center of that terrible and fierce storm was a tiny pinpoint of blue calm. That is where I have tried to put myself ever since my life changed."[14]

Beloved of God, you can avoid being blown away by the turbulent crises of life. You don't have to be pushed around by the winds of the world like a tumbleweed.

Instead, see yourself as an evergreen olive tree thriving in the presence of God, your roots deeply and broadly tangled in God's love and care, soaking in the nourishing waters of the Spirit.

See yourself in the "tiny pinpoint of blue calm" that is the very presence of God.

God, I want to stand strong, not in my own strength, not in any possessions or wealth or abilities or accomplishments, but in the security of your steadfast love. Today I will face numerous choices that will determine whether that happens. Help me choose wisely, because with each wise choice, my roots grow a little deeper.

Betrayed

THEMES
Friends
Betrayal
Relationships
Hurts
Disappointment

4 My heart is in anguish within me, the terrors of death have fallen upon me.

5 Fear and trembling come upon me, and horror overwhelms me. . . .

The feeling hits you like an electric shock. Your stomach feels like it's on fire, and your brain screams in disbelief. You simply can't believe what you just figured out, or read on a Facebook page, or heard from somebody who heard from somebody. It just can't be.

But it happened: Someone you thought you knew, someone you trusted, just stabbed you in the back. Someone you considered a close friend.

12 It is not enemies who taunt me—I could bear that; it is not adversaries who deal insolently with me—I could hide from them.

13 But it is you, my equal, my companion, my familiar friend,

14 with whom I kept pleasant company; we walked in the house of God with the throng. . . .

They shared a secret of yours you assumed was in the vault. They made fun of you with someone you were hoping to get to know better. They used your brilliant idea to impress the boss. They made up something about you that could almost be true but will surely get you in trouble with somebody sometime.

Why? Why would somebody you thought you knew do that to you?

A million thoughts rush through your brain. You want to hide, you're so embarrassed. You're angry. You want to get back at this so-called friend. You want to hurt him or her worse than he or she hurt you.

It's only natural. In fact, the psalm writer felt the exact way. He cried out to God when someone he thought he could trust totally betrayed him.

But somehow the psalmist starts to hear another inner voice: a reminder of God's love and support and understanding. And it's a reminder we all need to hear in times like this:

22 Cast your burden on the LORD, and he will sustain you; he will never permit the righteous to be moved.

Give it to God. Let God take the hurt and the anger and the humiliation, and God will carry you through it. Somehow.

But then there's that nagging reminder: "He will never permit the right-eous to be moved." The righteous one can stand up strong against anything. The righteous one won't get swept away in a flood of pain.

So how righteous am I? How careful have I been about what I've said about others–stretching the truth to be funny or hoping to get back at some-body with a story I never should have shared?

What kind of friend have I been?

Spend some time thinking about those questions. Start working at being the kind of friend you want your friends to be.

Yes, God, it hurts. That knife between my shoulder blades really cuts deep. And I don't deserve that. I'm as angry as the psalmist was about his betrayer–but I realize that anger doesn't help anybody. Help me forgive and move on. And open my eyes to the things I've said and done about others that may have hurt them, or made them mad, made them feel how I feel right now. Help me to be the kind of friend that wants the best for others. The kind of friend I want in my own life. Help me keep in mind that it's not all about me. It's about us. All of us.

Delivered

THEMES

Fear

Trust

Terror

Deliverance

Protection

Anxiety

2b O Most High,

3 when I am afraid, I put my trust in you.

4 In God, whose word I praise, in God I trust;
I am not afraid; what can flesh do to me? . . .

Not long ago I watched a 1961 movie I had never even heard of before: *The Roman Spring of Mrs. Stone*, with Vivien Leigh as an aging actress whose husband had unexpectedly died, leaving her alone in Rome, and Warren Beatty as an Italian gigolo. Based on a novella by Tennessee Williams and beautifully filmed in Rome, it is quite the extravagant soap opera.

The ending, however, is controversial because it's not clear what happens. In fact, you can take it two entirely different ways: On her balcony Vivien Leigh finally takes notice of a grungy but handsome beggar who has been surreptitiously stalking her throughout the movie, and tosses her room key down to him. As the man enters her apartment, we see him walk closer and closer. But does his expression indicate love, or malevolence? Would she finally experience fulfillment from her loneliness, or should she rather fear for her life? Is he the angel of death or the new love of her life? The viewer must decide.

I was so perplexed by the ending I watched the brief documentary about the film included on the DVD in hopes of an explanation. Some of the stars and experts interviewed were absolutely certain that their particular theory about the ending was the correct one, while others were as confused as I was.

One noted film expert and movie star biographer explained that he believed the film was actually about fear: Fear of growing old. Fear of being lonely and unloved. Fear of being taken advantage of. Fear of survival. Fear of being attacked on dark city streets. Fear of failure. Fear of fear! That hadn't occurred to me as I had watched the lush Technicolor production, but it made some sense.

So the film's ending—especially in the context of so much fear—could be taken as a life-threatening end, or it could be taken as a positive, hopeful, even loving resolution for a woman who had suffered so much fear and loneliness.

Then it occurred to me that the way one takes this ending depends on how one looks at life. If we live fearfully, we see threats in every corner. If we live openly, lovingly, trusting in God, maybe we can better see opportunities to love.

It all comes down to trust. Has your trust in life been shattered by fear? Or can you join with the psalmist in singing of your utter trust in God:

10 In God, whose word I praise, in the LORD, whose word I praise,

11 in God I trust; I am not afraid. What can a mere mortal do to me?

When we trust in God, we can move through life with confidence. We can be delivered from paralyzing fear–which gives us the freedom to love and to serve, to live in the light and share that light.

Naturally, we need to live wisely and carefully. We certainly shouldn't be foolish or naive, but rather alert to God at work all around us. When we do, we can live thankfully, joyfully, fully. And again we can sing with the psalmist:

12 My vows to you I must perform, O God; I will render thank offerings to you.

13 For you have delivered my soul from death, and my feet from falling, so that I may walk before God in the light of life.

God, it is so easy in this world to fall prey to fear. Yes, there are threats at every turn. But if I give in to that fear, I become paralyzed, self-protective, and small. Deliver me from my fear. Let me live in trust. Let me walk before you in the light of life. No fear. Just faith.

Awakened

Psalm 57

THEMES

Praise

Thankfulness

Awakening

Worship

Faithfulness

4 I lie down among lions that greedily devour human prey; their teeth are spears and arrows, their tongues sharp swords. . . .

Like you and I occasionally do (admit it!), the psalmist complains about those who have been mistreating him. They're after him with their teeth bared and arrows flying. They're like hungry lions just waiting to rip into their prey—the psalmist himself.

Sometimes those complaints are justified. What is one to do in the face of such opposition? Often there seems to be little choice.

When the mortgage foreclosure mess first gripped America in late 2008, one of the many distressing examples made national news: A ninety-year-old woman in Akron, Ohio, overwhelmed by the threat of losing the home she and her late husband had bought in 1970, shot herself twice with a shotgun as sheriff's deputies arrived to serve an eviction notice. She saw no other way out. The lions had apparently won.

However, her aim with that big shotgun was not so good and she survived the wounds. Her community—in fact, the whole nation—rallied around her, and her debt eventually was totally forgiven.[15]

In my life vicious opposition or fearful circumstances have never reached the point that I would want to aim a shotgun at my chest. But how would I respond if they did? Would I give up too?

6 They set a net for my steps; my soul was bowed down. They dug a pit in my path, but they have fallen into it themselves.

The psalmist prepared for the worst, but still he trusted God. Even though he hunkered down in fear, he relied on God to protect him. And in fact, his opponents fell into the very traps they'd set for him.

Whether the psalmist had fully escaped the threats he faced is unclear here, but what is clear is that he determines to rouse himself, to wake up and praise God no matter what—and loudly:

8 Awake, my soul! Awake, O harp and lyre! I will awake the dawn.

9 I will give thanks to you, O LORD, among the peoples; I will sing praises to you among the nations.

10 For your steadfast love is as high as the heavens; your faithfulness extends to the clouds.

In the face of treacherous conflict, the psalmist intends to snap out of it, to sing and play music to worship and praise God so exuberantly that he will "awake the dawn."

In the midst of his difficulties he knows—deep down—that God's love and faithfulness toward him are steadfast, immense, overpowering. And so he praises God:

> 11 *Be exalted, O God, above the heavens. Let your glory be over all the earth.*

Are you cowering in fear of your circumstances? Wake up. Snap out of it. Become alert to who God is and what God is doing in your life. And start singing.

God, in the midst of my fearful doldrums, sound the alarm clock in my soul. I don't want to give in to my panic. I want to be awake and alert and alive, focused on you and all you are doing, with and to and for and through me. I want to praise you every moment of the day—no matter what I will face.

Angered

Psalm 58

THEMES
Evil
Violence
Justice
Vengeance
Righteousness

It seems people can hardly have a discussion involving politics, religion, world events, culture, or any number of other hot-button subjects today without it devolving into an attack against the other. To some extent I blame the media for much of the vitriol we are bombarded with day after day—one-sided talk radio, the television news panel discussions that become so fiery at times, the scorched-earth methods employed by many political campaigns. In this world it seems you have to choose sides, stick to your guns no matter what, and yell louder than the other person.

A glance at the headlines reveals that political or religious differences can often end in violence—not only in the hot spots of the world, where religion clashes against religion and ethnic group wars against ethnic group, but in neighborhoods and workplaces and sometimes even schools and churches.

Perhaps it has always been this way. People of pretty much any religion have often considered themselves the sole possessors of the truth, and contend that those who disagree are either ignorant or wicked. The psalmist was so incensed by the apparent enemies of God surrounding him that he begged God to destroy them:

> *6 O God, break the teeth in their mouths; tear out the fangs of the young lions, O LORD!*
>
> *7 Let them vanish like water that runs away; like grass let them be trodden down and wither.*
>
> *8 Let them be like the snail that dissolves into slime; like the untimely birth that never sees the sun. . . .*

Yes, the psalmist is upset with the "wicked." That's an understatement. He says they lie, they sting, they hurt, they deceive, and they do all that from the moment they come out of the womb.

But, let's be real: Who are the "wicked"? Aren't they just people like us? Confused, scared, hurting, just like you and me?

A bank ran a controversial commercial illustrating this situation:

Protesters guard a stand of trees, preventing a team of loggers from advancing. The police arrive and forcibly wrest the protesters from the forest. One young woman, her hands zip-tied behind her back, glares at a bald logger as she's led to a police cruiser. "Are you happy now?" she asks. Cut to a small jail. The woman is released from a cell, having been bailed out by the bald logger. She leaves the jail in a huff and gets on a motorcycle. The bald logger follows her out–and gets on the same motorcycle. As they drive along a woodland road, the woman, who has been holding on to a rear handlebar, puts her arms around the waist of the logger, who smiles almost imperceptibly. A narrator says: "The more you look at the world, the more you recognize that people value things differently."[16]

Though I'm not sure what this has to do with banking, the message is clear: The man and woman obviously have different values and are willing to stand up for them. But their relationship is the most important thing.

That seems to me a godly goal, a lesson worth learning. And yet, here in the Bible is a violent condemnation of those who are different. And the rhetoric troubles me deeply:

10 The righteous will rejoice when they see vengeance done; they will bathe their feet in the blood of the wicked.

Isn't this part of the problem? Name-calling and pledges of violence, even in the name of God? So what do we do with Scripture passages like this?

Maybe we let them disturb us, shake us up. Maybe we wrestle with them. Maybe we look at ourselves in them, as a mirror. Maybe we search our own hearts for such violent emotions against others who disagree with us, or look different from us, or express their faith in other ways than we do.

Maybe we let these psalms purge us of the violent thoughts within our own hearts and minds, and cause us to stop and think and reflect on who the other is and why they are as they are, and how we can somehow come together and even be in relationship with one another.

Maybe we ask ourselves just whose side God is on–or does God even take sides?

11 People will say, "Surely there is a reward for the righteous; surely there is a God who judges on earth."

Here is the point: Ultimately, God will put an end to violence and injustice. Differences will become the wisp of a forgotten nightmare. Pain and oppression will evaporate under God's perfect judgment.

Ultimately. But what could you do or say today, in God's righteous and loving strength, to take a step in that direction?

God, if I'm honest I admit I get as angered as anyone does about differences in politics or religion or whatever the issue may be. But help me get clear that you are the Judge, not me. You are the one who will deal with what's wicked, not me. Keep me aware of the times today when I cross the line. Give me the wisdom and strength to be a peacemaker in your name. Give me the heart to know that we are all in this together.

Staggered

Psalm 60

THEMES
Trials
Troubles
Reaction
Response
Trust
Hope

2 [O God,][y]ou have caused the land to quake;
you have torn it open; repair the cracks in it, for
it is tottering.

3 You have made your people suffer hard things;
you have given us wine to drink that made us reel.

Not long ago I accompanied a friend to dinner with several people he had worked with years earlier. They had kept in touch over the years but rarely had had the chance to get together. As you can imagine, with all the catching-up and reminiscing, there was much laughing, tale-telling, and good humor. As a newcomer to these longtime friendships, I marveled at how easy and fun and loyal they all were, despite the time and distance that separated them. We laughed until it hurt and that felt good.

It wasn't until the next day that the thought struck me that every person around that table had suffered incredibly in the past few years.

One had, along with her family, had to make the excruciating decision to pull the plug on a beloved family member who, after nearly a year in a coma, had no hope of resuscitation.

Another had had two back surgeries and still wrestled with health issues, causing her to have to sell her beloved retail business because she could no longer handle the physical responsibilities.

Two of them had come through difficult divorces and were still coping with all the fallout and trying to rebuild their lives.

One had recently lost another beloved family member and mentor at a far too early age.

All of us were struggling with various financial issues, family responsibilities, work pressures, health fears . . . on and on. There were times in recent years that each one of us had reeled from the earthquakes that had shaken our lives, experiencing emotional and physical pain from all those problems. At times we could easily have cried out with the writer of this psalm.

And yet, you could hardly have imagined all those painful scenarios from the grand and glorious time we had around the dinner table.

It's true: All of us will pass through seasons of pain and confusion and fear, weeping through dark nights and praying for some dim light at the dawn. We stagger from the wine we've been given to drink, the trials and turmoils that leave us dazed by confusion and a lack of control.

The painful arrows of life rain down on us. How do we react? How should we respond? We trust in God. And we pray with the psalmist:

4 You have set up a banner for those who fear you, to rally to it out of bowshot.

5 Give victory with your right hand, and answer us, so that those whom you love may be rescued.

During our conversation in the noisy restaurant, my friend remembered a quotation that he'd found helpful in such times: "I am convinced that life is 10 percent what happens to me and 90 percent how I react to it."[17]

That may be oversimplistic. And the math may not be exactly right. But it does help us understand that we cannot let ourselves be victimized by our circumstances, or staggered by the ramifications of our choices in life. We can trust that we will get through this, that we can run to God's banner and find rescue.

God, I don't want to minimize what I'm going through. I don't want to pretend that it's not important and it's not huge. I don't want to act as though it doesn't matter, because it does, and it will for a long time. But I also don't want to stagger and reel in confusion and fear and anger over it. I want to trust you. I want to struggle through it, deal with it responsibly, learn from it, and rise above it. And I know that I can only do that with you.

Sheltered

THEMES

Protection

Fear

Powerlessness

Transcendence

Creation

¹ Hear my cry, O God; listen to my prayer.

² From the end of the earth I call to you, when my heart is faint. Lead me to the rock that is higher than I;

The psalmist found himself at "the end of the earth." He was backed into a corner with nowhere to run. He felt he had run out of room to move. And he cried to God.

There are times when we too feel we are at the end of our rope. At the end of our very existence. We are inundated by fear or faintheartedness; our faith is shallow and we feel attacked on all sides by bitter circumstances or threats. And there seems to be no way to move forward without drowning in pain.

When we face an "end of the earth" experience like that, how can we turn it into one of beauty and peace, acknowledging God's power over what lies beyond that end?

When the psalmist felt he was at his end, utterly spent, entirely used up, he turned to God, asking God to raise him up to safety on the strong, unshakable, solid rock of God's presence. He couldn't climb up there on his own. God had to lead him there, pull him up, set him high.

³ for you are my refuge, a strong tower against the enemy.

⁴ Let me abide in your tent forever, find refuge under the shelter of your wings.

God is our rock above the stormy sea. God is our refuge, a strong, solid tower of safety and security. God is our peaceful tent of worship and meditation. God's wings of protection give us safe shelter.

Rather than feeling cornered or stuck with no room to move, we can see ourselves in a different place—and marvel at God's sheltering power in that place. It can look as if we have no options for going forward, but that's when God can act. The end of the earth can be the beginning of a new direction. And we can move forward in the sheltering protection of God.

Once, literally, I found myself at the "end of the earth," and it was a much different experience. A friend and I visited St. Joseph Peninsula State Park in Florida on the Gulf of Mexico many years ago. We set up a tent in the campgrounds and spent a leisurely day on the oddly deserted beach. We'd seen on a map that the peninsula stretched more than seven miles into the gulf, and decided to walk to the very end. After a couple of hours or so, admiring the surf and the sand dunes, the gulls and crabs, the flotsam and jetsam that had washed up on the white sand shore, we made it to the end— the end of the earth as far as we were concerned. We stared out into the peaceful, crisp blue waters of the gulf for a few moments, congratulating God on the handiwork we'd marveled at. And then we turned around and walked back into the real world with a sense of joyful calm.

When I face an "end of the earth" experience as the psalmist did, I try to remember this experience. Rather than feeling trapped, I want to remember the openness, the peace, and the beauty of that peninsula. And when I can't seem to move forward one more step, I want to remember that it's time to look up and trust God.

You may find yourself standing still and feeling powerless at the end of the earth, but you can be there in the sheltering presence of God. You can see your circumstances more clearly and realize how powerless they are over you. You can marvel at the extreme beauty and peace surrounding you. You can see God in it. And you can know God through it.

God, sometimes I do feel that I am at my end, spent and used up. There is nowhere else to go. One more step and I will fall off into the darkness or drown in the hopelessness. Pull me up, God. Set me on a solid foundation, shelter me, and surround me with your strong wings. And let me abide with you in that place forever so I can move forward in your new direction.

Silenced

THEMES

Rest

Quiet

Trust

Turmoil

Hope

Refuge

1 For God alone my soul waits in silence; from him comes my salvation.

2 He alone is my rock and my salvation, my fortress; I shall never be shaken. . . .

When I lived in a condo on the ground floor in the middle of Midtown Atlanta, traffic noises were constant. Just outside the French doors to the patio, boisterous groups of people would walk by on the way to or from one of the many dining spots and watering holes nearby. Raucous Pride Parades rolled by once a year. Hundreds or even thousands of runners in a 10K race or a marathon or a charity walk moved by, cheered on by onlookers. And on top of all that, I lived directly across from Fire Station No. 15.

So, yes, despite the pleasantness of this place, it could get a little noisy at times. To help me sleep at night, I had a white noise machine, and occasionally I'd even stuff some earplugs in my ears. I craved the quiet.

In some ways, I got used to all the noise. Before I moved into this condo, I spoke with an Episcopal priest who lived on the top floor of the building. How was it living in this condo complex, I asked? He replied, "Well, the first night I moved in, five years ago, I thought, 'Oh no, I have made a horrible mistake.' The fire truck sirens woke me up with a jolt in the middle of the night, and twice more before dawn. But I found that within three nights, I had adjusted and I've never been awakened by the sirens again."

Though it took me four nights to get to that point, he was absolutely right. Which is a little scary. We can get so used to the constant roaring noise of life that we tune it all out, pay no attention. We just zone out. I'm always amazed at how many people walk or run around with earbuds stuffed in their ears, listening to music to distract them from where they are in the moment.

But the psalmist reminds us that, if we're not careful, we can miss out on something that can be soul-nurturing: waiting in silence for God.

The psalmist was assailed by battering assailants who were trying to take him down (v. 3). It sounds very noisy and frightening. Yet somehow he was able to wait in silence for God, to wait in trust and hope.

The truth is, it's difficult to hear God speak healing words to us when the noise of life and conflict buffets our souls. God's is a still, small voice, an unmistakable whisper. And we must quiet ourselves to hear it.

The psalmist was able to do that. He knew he had to if he was going to hold on to hope. But he also had to wait for it.

5 For God alone my soul waits in silence, for my hope is from him. . . .

What are the noises in your life—the racket that disturbs you, the sounds you use to protect yourself from hearing what you are afraid to hear? Why are you afraid of the quiet? What do you think you'll hear?

Find a quiet place and wrestle with those questions. That quiet place is within you, wherever you are, whatever is passing by outside your room. It is a place of trust in the midst of the raucous turmoil. A place of quiet hope and restful refuge. A place where you can commune with God in utter honesty. A place where you can hear God whisper your name. You too may need to wait for it, but it's sure to be worth it.

8 Trust in him at all times, O people; pour out your heart before him;
God is a refuge for us.

God, right now as I write this, I hear a pair of mourning doves chant. I hear a crow caw. I hear the beeping backing-up warning of a dump truck. I hear a car swoosh by. I hear the refrigerator motor turn on and whine. And yet I also hear the silence of refuge. The quiet of trust. Let me also hear your voice. I wait in silence.

Watered

THEMES

Thirstiness

Thriving

Abundance

Provision

Enrichment

Drought

5 By awesome deeds you answer us with deliverance,
O God of our salvation; you are the hope of all the
ends of the earth and of the farthest seas.

6 By your strength you established the mountains;
you are girded with might.

7 You silence the roaring of the seas, the roaring of their waves,
the tumult of the peoples. . . .

The southeastern United States, where I live, was plagued by a drought in recent years. The man-made lakes of North Georgia revealed hideous scars of red clay around the banks because the water level was so low. Mandatory watering restrictions were implemented, so there were lots of dirty cars and empty flowerbeds around. The large city park canceled all the major events typically held there—the Dogwood arts and crafts festival, the Peachtree 10K Road Race finish line, the Atlanta Pride celebration—sending them to mall parking lots or the Atlanta Civic Center. The governor of Georgia even held a prayer meeting on the steps of the state capitol, begging God for rain, but it was several months before a few showers reluctantly fell.

Even with spring storms the waterfall deficit seemed impossible to make up. The Georgia legislature even tried to invade the southeastern corner of Tennessee, claiming the border between the states had been incorrectly drawn for two centuries. Of course, the enlarged border would have taken in a piece of the Tennessee River, giving the parched state of Georgia another water source to drain.

The cause of this water shortage seems to be twofold. Not only had there been a consistent rainfall deficit over several years, but developers had also been expanding the construction of housing subdivisions and commercial centers exponentially, creating a fast-growing need for an ever-shrinking water supply. So we can blame both nature and humanity for the problem.

Despite all the dire warnings and pleas for conservation, not much has changed in the way of our behavior. Oh, we may turn the water off while we brush our teeth, take shorter showers, and avoid watering our lawns. But, deep down, we assume it will all work out and we'll eventually be able to open the spigots full force. It's really not that serious. Besides, as this psalm points out:

9 You visit the earth and water it, you greatly enrich it; the river of God is full of water; you provide the people with grain, for so you have prepared it.

10 You water its furrows abundantly, settling its ridges, softening it with showers, and blessing its growth.

So, is God not doing a good job with the watering provision here? Well, in recent months rain showers have returned and lake levels are rising, so I suppose eventually it will all work out—God does provide. But we still need to address the human issues regarding the overuse and abuse of our precious water supplies.

God may be the source of water, and of all our resources, but that's no reason to take it for granted. We are called to be stewards and caretakers of creation. We have to work with God on this, and not simply expect God to come through with whatever it is we think we need, especially when our need is the result of our carelessness or greed.

By the way, this attitude applies not only to our natural world, but also to our spiritual life. God is able to release the floodgates of abundant blessing and provision, enabling us to thrive. But we have to work with God. Preparing the fields. Caring for the garden. Harvesting the bounty:

11 You crown the year with your bounty; your wagon tracks overflow with richness.

Perhaps a little wise care on our part can help end the spiritual drought we're experiencing. Then God can water our furrows, work our hard edges, soften our crusted heart, shower us with joy, and bless our growth.

God, I'm dry. I've been dry for a while. I will believe in your promise to provide the water of the Spirit to refresh me, so I can produce a fragrant and nourishing garden of spiritual gifts. I will prepare the fallow ground of my heart and care for it tenderly, so that when the waters come, I'll be ready.

Tested

THEMES
Trials
Tests
Praise
Struggles
Cleansing
Purity

8 Bless our God, O peoples, let the sound of his praise be heard,

9 who has kept us among the living, and has not let our feet slip.

10 For you, O God, have tested us; you have tried us as silver is tried.

Precious metals such as silver are subjected to intense heat in order to purify them. Using a blast of flame the skilled silversmith can skim out impurities in the molten metal so it becomes even more precious and pure, ready to be molded into something beautiful, something that shines even brighter.

The psalmist reveals that that is the process through which the people of God often go. And it can hurt.

11 You brought us into the net; you laid burdens on our backs;

12 you let people ride over our heads; we went through fire and through water; yet you have brought us out to a spacious place. . . .

Yes, God tests us with a refining fire in order to purify us. What's more, God lays the burden on us, lets people run over us at times, and takes us through fire and water. Sounds like great fun, doesn't it?

But if we can keep in mind, even in the midst of the harsh trials of our lives, that our trustworthy God is the One who's at work, then maybe we can get through these times with our sanity intact, and perhaps even with praises on our lips. Because in the end, we can trust that God will take us to a "spacious place," a land of promise, a life of wholeness.

Think about the circumstance you're struggling with right now. The aches and pains of life that only seem to get worse the more you try to remedy them. The surprise attacks your circumstances are making on you from every side. You may not have a clue as to what God is doing in all this, where God is leading you. All you know is that you're trusting God. And perhaps, you're even praising God in the midst of it all, because you know God's love for you is unwavering:

20 Blessed be God, because he has not rejected my prayer or removed his steadfast love from me.

Between the time I write this and the time you read this, my life may have turned upside down. It has in the past, so it probably will again. After all, when I look back over the past decade of my life I can see plenty of fires of struggle and tribulation that have burned me, one after another. Some of them were admittedly self-inflicted, while others simply crashed into life with no forewarning.

Even so, I got through them all. And I think—I hope—I learned something from each flame, allowing it to do its work in my soul.

In these dark times of struggle and pain, when we least feel like singing God's praises, keep this psalm in mind:

Maybe God is testing us, refining us under the fire as silver is tested and cleansed.

Maybe this is yet another attempt of God to cleanse us from our selfish ways, our deceitful tricks, our inauthentic habits, our baseless fears.

Maybe God is turning up the heat, but God isn't going to let our feet slip in the lava.

And maybe, just maybe, we can thank God for that.

Wherever you are in this process, when you feel like you're worthless and far from glittering silver, keep in mind that at least you are silver ore. You're worth something. Otherwise, God would not bother turning up the heat in order to clean us up and make us shine.

God, if the heat I'm experiencing is coming from you, please use it to cleanse me. Let the impurities in my heart and soul bubble up so you can examine them, remove them, and make me into something that reflects you in even brighter ways.

Blessed

THEMES

Blessing

Encourage-
ment

Acceptance

Love

Sharing

1 May God be gracious to us and bless us and make his face to shine upon us,

2 that your way may be known upon earth, your saving power among all nations. . . .

Many of us struggle with our self-worth. We hunger for acceptance, encouragement, and love. We yearn to receive a blessing—a momentous expression of loving approval and appreciation.

Whether it comes from a parent, teacher, mentor, boss, or some other significant person in our lives, we can thrive when we sense this blessing—and we can plummet to the depths of despair if, despite all our efforts to please, we never receive it.

Not long ago, I received a blessing that moved me deeply. For the last year and a half of his life, my strong, robust, active father existed on his back in a nursing home bed, fighting his failing body and mind, struggling against the dementia that continued to darken his memory. Yet, somehow, a wall of reservation crumbled as well, because he began to make a habit of expressing—extravagantly—his love and encouragement to his family and friends at just about every opportunity.

My dad had been a highly regarded United Methodist minister in West Virginia. He was the best preacher I think I have ever heard, though as a kid I didn't appreciate that. I think the public nature of his role took its toll on him at times, as he tended to be naturally introverted. That meant he could be a bit irritable at home, and I now realize that was because he was depleted and had to deal with four rowdy kids. On many levels I understand and identify with him now. In fact, often when I look in the mirror, I wonder, what is Dad doing in my mirror?

Over those last eighteen months of his life, following a toxic shock reaction to an infection that nearly killed him, my brothers and I would make the trip home as often as we could; our sister lived nearby and checked on him daily. Often our conversations with him grew frustrating as the dementia caused him to talk nonsense as though it made perfect sense. Early on we tried to correct his babblings and help him understand the reality, but after a while we learned to let him go and just go with him. But no, we never found the multimillion dollars of Chinese money hidden under the basement steps he assured us were there.

Sometimes, though, he was lucid and positive, and he would ask insightful questions about what was going on with us and offer encouragement. One day, about six months before he passed away, I happened to be alone with him in his nursing home room. I sat on the edge of his bed and he took my hands in his parchment-skinned, trembling hands—the ones that had always seemed so big and strong to me—and looked me deep in my eyes. And he said in his quavering, deep voice, "Pete, I want you to know, I love you, I am so proud of you. You are my son in whom I am well pleased—*well* pleased."

Tears flooded my eyes. I may have been over fifty at the time, but I felt like a blessed child. I'm sure I had frustrated and upset my father innumerable times over those years. Lots of disappointments. Lots of hurts and pains and difficulties. And yet . . . "You are my son in whom I am well pleased—*well* pleased."

It was a blessing only a parent can give to a child, and I realized in that moment that so many, many children never hear such words of love and encouragement from their parents. It is a rare gift indeed. And it sank deep within my body and mind and soul and still resonates there today, more than two years after he died.

All of us hunger for this encouragement, this blessing. We want so desperately to be accepted and loved. And whether we realize it or not, God offers this to us continually. The psalmist asked for God's blessing, and we can make this our prayer as well: *"May God be gracious to us and bless us and make his face to shine upon us . . ."*

Pray that right now. Realize it. Experience it. Soak it up.

But don't stop there. There's a purpose for that blessing, for that filling up on encouragement, love, and acceptance: *". . . that your way may be known upon the earth, your saving power among all nations."*

See, we're supposed to share the blessing. We're supposed to receive God's blessing and then turn around and share it with those around us. And by doing so, we make God known on the earth. We share God's saving power among all.

Imagine a world where people blessed one another in this way.

It starts with God. Goes to you. Now where?

7 May God continue to bless us; let all the ends of the earth revere him.

God, I praise you for blessing me with your love and acceptance. Empower me to bless others, to speak words of encouragement, perform acts of peace and reconciliation, and help create opportunities for your love to break out.

Strengthened

THEMES
Strength
Protection
Care
Loss
Need
Weakness
Provision

4 Sing to God, sing praises to his name; lift up a song to him who rides upon the clouds—his name is the Lord—be exultant before him.

5 Father of orphans and protector of widows is God in his holy habitation.

6 God gives the desolate a home to live in; he leads out the prisoners to prosperity, but the rebellious live in a parched land. . . .

My father died six months after my mother did, so peacefully and "finally." When my brothers and sister and I were together for Dad's funeral, we expressed what we all felt in spite of the fact that we were all functioning adults in our fifties: Now we're orphans.

Of course, our circumstances hardly compared with the world's widows and orphans who face catastrophe on top of their grief and loss. They are far more vulnerable and needy than we. Even so, we felt the emptiness of those who no longer have their parents to love and care for them.

These verses come in a rousing psalm of jubilant praise for the God who has brought the nation of Israel successfully through battle against their enemies. There's a lot of tumult and blood in this psalm, but in the midst of it is this jewel of insight into the character of God, the "father of orphans and protector of widows." And it's worth admiring, because it can assure you that whatever losses you find yourself dealing with, God promises to care for you:

- *"Father of orphans."* If you feel confused and alone, not sure where to go next in life, God can lovingly parent you. Whether your human parents are alive or not, God offers the wisdom and encouragement you need. *Let God be your parent.*

- *"Protector of widows."* If you have lost an important relationship with a spouse or partner, whether through death or separation, God can protect you, make you feel at home, guide you through your grief, give you hope for what's next. *Let God be your lover.*

- *"God gives the desolate a home."* If you feel homeless, rootless, without a support system, God can guide you into a new family, a worshiping community of faith, love, and service. *Let God be your dwelling.*

- *"God leads out the prisoners to prosperity."* If you feel imprisoned by financial stresses, job frustrations, and unwanted responsibilities, trapped by poverty or depression or fear, God can bring you into prosperity—not necessarily financial, but emotional and spiritual, which is far more important. *Let God be your redeemer.*

This is why you can praise God along with the psalmist. You can see God for who God is, so you can sing.

But God doesn't expect you to do this on your own, out of your own meager resources. The psalmist continues:

28 Summon your might, O God; show your strength, O God, as you have done for us before.

The translation of that first phrase unfortunately hides a glorious truth. As one contemporary translation puts it: "Your God has decided you will be strong."[18]

See the difference? Yes, God can, with a divine and mighty zap, simply change things. But perhaps instead God has summoned the power for you, provided you with the strength you need to overcome the circumstances you find yourself in, as an orphan, a widow or widower, homeless, a prisoner—whether those circumstances are physical, emotional, or spiritual.

God has given you all the strength, hope, and wisdom you need to rise above the lonely, dark place you find yourself in. God has "decided you will be strong," beckoning you to push and risk and stretch the limits of your faith.

Even when you're empty and alone and stuck, even when you feel orphaned, God has given you the power to step forward in hope and praise.

God, if you've given me the power I need to overcome this loss I'm struggling with, this need for care and protection and family, then let me tap into it. Let me take the next step in faith, push the limits, take the risk, and see what happens.

Mired

Psalm 69

———

THEMES

Humiliation
Shame
Trust
Rescue
Deliverance

*¹ Save me, O God, for the waters have come up to
my neck.*

*² I sink in deep mire, where there is no foothold;
I have come into deep waters, and the flood sweeps
over me.*

Two nine-year-old boys were playing in a quarry in the United Kingdom. One stepped into quicksand and the other tried to rescue him, but both got caught in the thick slurry. One boy, Harry, explained: "We struggled to get out for about twenty minutes before Dale phoned his mum for help as it had reached our bellies. While we were waiting we both started to pray. We were so cold and I wasn't sure if we'd ever be found. I thought we were going to die." The mother frantically called police, then tried to call her son back—but the phone just kept ringing. They had sunk up to their necks. "You can imagine what I was thinking," she said. "I was so distraught. I honestly thought they'd both gone under." Thankfully, the boys were rescued just in time and learned an important lesson. The mother, who got there as quickly as she could, said, "It felt like forever before the police and the firemen turned up, but it could only have been ten minutes."[19]

You know that feeling. For whatever reason, you find yourself sinking deeper and deeper in the waters. The mud. The mire. The quicksand. There's no way to pull yourself out. And you're up to your neck in it.

*³ I am weary with my crying; my throat is parched. My eyes grow dim
with waiting for my God. . . .*

You're so tired of feeling trapped, so weary of screaming and weeping about it, that the thought of letting go and going under comes easily. But you pray, one more time. "Save me, O God. . . ."

And still you wait for rescue. You feel you now know what eternity is all about, because nothing changes day after day, except for the fact that you've sunk a little deeper while you wait.

You know it's the result of your own choices, your own stubbornness. That only makes it all the more shameful. And you know God knows all about it.

*⁵ O God, you know my folly; the wrongs I have done are not hidden
from you.*

6 Do not let those who hope in you be put to shame because of me,
O Lord God of hosts; do not let those who seek you be dishonored
because of me, O God of Israel. . . .

You're supposed to have it together. You've led people to believe that you know God and trust God, that you can be trusted. That you're honest and good and helpful. And now this. What will people think? Not only about you, but about this God you're supposed to believe in?

You continue waiting, sinking, and wondering how this is all going to come out. How big of an embarrassment it all is. How bad of a mess you'll have left behind.

13 But as for me, my prayer is to you, O Lord. At an acceptable time,
O God, in the abundance of your steadfast love, answer me. With your
faithful help
14 rescue me from sinking in the mire; let me be delivered from my ene-
mies and from the deep waters. . . .

As you keep waiting, do you keep trusting? Do you still hope and pray that God will make something out of this? It may stink. It may look really bad. But maybe you can learn something from it. Maybe you can grow a little through it. Maybe, who knows, you can help someone else going through the same awful thing.

17 Do not hide your face from your servant, for I am in distress—make
haste to answer me.
18 Draw near to me, redeem me, set me free . . .

Keep praying. Keep waiting. Keep trusting. The acceptable time for deliverance will come. God will come near, redeem you, pull you out, and set you free. And maybe you will be a better person as a result.

God, there's nothing more terrifying than the feeling of helpless immobility in the midst of a horrible situation. And that's where I am right now, crying, pleading, waiting for you. And trusting you.

Surrounded

THEMES
Community
Deliverance
Support
Love
Family
Friends

1 Be pleased, O God, to deliver me. O LORD, make haste to help me! . . .

4 Let all who seek you rejoice and be glad in you. Let those who love your salvation say evermore, "God is great!"

5 But I am poor and needy; hasten to me, O God! You are my help and my deliverer; O LORD, do not delay!

One of my favorite television series lasted only a few weeks on air before it was yanked—presumably because of low ratings but obviously because of the religious controversy it stirred. *The Book of Daniel* was created by Jack Kenny and starred Aidan Quinn as the Reverend Daniel Webster, an Episcopal priest who had to deal with a variety of desperate circumstances and quirky characters.

I've watched all eight episodes produced, most of which never aired, on the compilation DVD. In episode seven, entitled "God's Will," Daniel and his family must cope with a son who's in the hospital hovering near death after a brutal street beating at the hands of antigay bigots. If anyone could pray the prayer of this psalm then, it was the Reverend Webster.

And yet, in the aftermath of that horrific time of fear and pain that he and his family endured, he stood in the pulpit on a Sunday morning and preached to his flock:

> It's always darkest before the dawn. Not really true, but something we rely on so that maybe we'll fear the darkness a little bit less. . . . God gives us no burden that [God] thinks we cannot shoulder. With the help of a wife, a husband, a partner, with children, family, friends, with community and with faith, our shoulders become many. The weight diminishes. And this is God's will, that we live for each other. That we forgive impossible transgressions. That in spite of what some might see as the never-ending circus of horrors that roll on beyond these walls, we look within ourselves to find beauty and hope and the dawn that always arrives to push the darkness away. And that dawn, that light, comes from love.[20]

This priest is on to something. Did you notice that verse in the middle of the short, frantic prayer for rescue and deliverance in this psalm? *"Let all who seek you rejoice and be glad in you. Let those who love your salvation say evermore, 'God is great!'"* That's the key. We need all of us to survive. Seeking, rejoicing, being glad, loving, speaking truth—together.

This tells me something very important: We not only need to speak our deepest needs to God, to converse with him in utterly honest ways, but we also need the community of faith to do so fully. For through the love and care of the body of believers, God often provides the deliverance we so desperately crave.

This is what living in faith as a follower of God is all about. It's doing it together, in love. Offering beauty and hope to others who desperately need it, knowing that when it's your time to need it, it will be there in abundance in the community of faith.

Who in your life can you turn to for support when you are desperately in need of rescue?

Whose burden do you in turn need to help shoulder today?

God, I know I tend to get focused on myself and my own needs, and so often get stuck there. Remind me that I am part of a family—a faith community, a network of friends, perhaps even my own family. And remind me that that support system is designed by you to provide me with help from others, and to provide others with help from me. I rejoice in that gift from your hands.

Nurtured

THEMES
Childhood
Tradition
Faith
Trust
Youth
Care

⁴ Rescue me, O my God, from the hand of the wicked, from the grasp of the unjust and cruel.

⁵ For you, O Lord, are my hope, my trust, O LORD, from my youth.

⁶ Upon you I have leaned from my birth; it was you who took me from my mother's womb. My praise is continually of you. . . .

When you look back over your life, from your earliest memories to today, do you see evidences of God's love and nurture?

As you page through old family scrapbooks or watch old family videos, do you see the child you were as one who was blessed by God? Or was your childhood marked by so much fear and pain you had no notion of God's care?

After my folks passed away, my brother Greg gave me a CD containing a whole slew of family photos that he had found in various cabinets and drawers at our folks' home and then scanned. There were some photos of us kids that I don't remember seeing.

I look at the young child I was then, the third son of four children, and I wish I could speak to him. Tell him all will be well. Encourage him to seek to follow God without fear. Beg him to trust the love that surrounded him.

But one thing is unmistakable as I look at those images of time caught on film, digitized, and displayed with crisp clarity on my laptop screen: I was loved. Not only by my parents but also by God. And I knew it.

Even now I can recall so many instances of that love . . .

I grew up in a family who went to church pretty much every time the doors opened; naturally, because my Dad was the pastor. This was in the day of Wednesday and Sunday evening services, and choir practice for kids. Vacation Bible School. Methodist Youth Fellowship. Youth choir tours and pageants. It was always a very active church life.

I remember sitting with my little sister Ann with Mrs. Melton during Sunday morning services, because Dad was up front and Mom was in the choir. Mrs. Melton, one of the sweetest souls I've known, would bring us Life Savers candy rolls and pads of blank paper, and Ann and I would sit there quietly and create comic books and odes to the Beatles and whatever else our childishly creative minds could summon. I still have a dozen or so of those illustrated pads in a cigar box somewhere.

I remember in high school when my friend Allyson and I led a discussion about Christian themes in pop music for, of all people, the women's circle. We played records like "Bridge over Troubled Waters" by Simon and Garfunkel and knowingly explained how that could be about Jesus.

I remember dreading having to go to choir practice, but cherishing that fact now because I love church music so much. I can still sing along to some of the all-choir cantatas our choir director couple, the McDowells, rehearsed us for over and over again. We sang some great hymns lustily, surely making Charles Wesley proud.

Many memories, and I am thankful for all the nurture I received from the moment I was born. And now I pray a new prayer—one I know God will answer:

17 O God, from my youth you have taught me, and I still proclaim your wondrous deeds.

18 So even to old age and gray hairs, O God, do not forsake me, until I proclaim your might to all the generations to come.

From the womb until now, God has never let loose of me. I pray—I know—that it only will get better and better with age.

No matter how old you are, no matter what your spiritual upbringing involved, I hope you know that too.

God, I want to take some time and think back over some of my early memories, and see you at work in them. I want to appreciate the ways you nurtured and guided me over the years, through so many people who cared. Now please give me creativity and wisdom to see whom I can help sense your love and care in their young years.

Reminded

Psalm 74

THEMES
Enemies
Attack
Impatience
Authority
Defeat
Trust

1 O God, why do you cast us off forever? Why does your anger smoke against the sheep of your pasture?

2 Remember your congregation, which you acquired long ago, which you redeemed to be the tribe of your heritage. Remember Mount Zion, where you came to dwell.

3 Direct your steps to the perpetual ruins; the enemy has destroyed everything in the sanctuary. . . .

The psalmist isn't happy. On behalf of the nation, he feels abandoned by God, forgotten and lost. Why is God so angry with them, the poor sheep of God's pasture? Their enemies have won—they've taken over and destroyed the holy places of God. These enemies continually scoff at God and revile God's name, shaming the downtrodden people of God, and God does nothing—nothing!—despite their pleas. And the psalmist is not happy about it.

But in the midst of all this despair and frustration come these verses, which put things into context:

12 Yet God my King is from of old, working salvation in the earth.

13 You divided the sea by your might; you broke the heads of the dragons in the waters.

14 You crushed the heads of Leviathan; you gave him as food for the creatures of the wilderness.

15 You cut openings for springs and torrents; you dried up ever-flowing streams.

These beautiful words remind us who is really in charge. God can do anything God wants. God is working salvation in this old planet, a world that God worked and molded and formed. The seas, the creatures, the springs, the sun and the moon and stars, the seasons and all the blessings they bring—all came from the Creator's hand.

So if God can do all that, then God can put those foes in their place—in God's good time.

16 Yours is the day, yours also the night; you established the luminaries and the sun.

17 You have fixed all the bounds of the earth; you made summer and winter.

God is the ultimate power. Everything created has come from the hand of God. Reminding ourselves of this truth—while we're waiting for whatever deliverance we seek—will put things into perspective and empower us to wait for that deliverance.

Sometimes it helps to take these verses literally, and take the time to enjoy and experience God's world. I had an hour's walk this dazzling spring morning, the sky intensely blue, azaleas and pear trees and assorted flowers exploding all around me. I walked by the ocean, observing the waves curling and crashing on ancient sand, seagulls swooping for breakfast, children running into the foam, lovers walking hand in hand. I walked by the peaceful green marsh veined by meandering streams, watching fallen leaves floating in the lazy waterway.

It's all part of life, part of creation. Seeing it puts things into perspective and reminds me that God can do this. God can do anything. Why am I so impatient for it?

God, I can identify with the psalmist, who seems frustrated and anxious while waiting for you to act. I know you're there. I know you're able. I know, deep down, that you will do what you will do when you will do it. You always have, you always will. So while I wait, enable me to experience, appreciate, and enjoy your handiwork.

Troubled

THEMES
Depression
Comfort
Exhaustion
Meditation
Remembering

1 I cry aloud to God, aloud to God, that he may hear me.

2 In the day of my trouble I seek the Lord; in the night my hand is stretched out without wearying; my soul refuses to be comforted.

3 I think of God, and I moan; I meditate, and my spirit faints.

4 You keep my eyelids from closing; I am so troubled that I cannot speak.

Sleeplessness has created a number of successful industries. A whole variety of solutions are available for those who suffer from insomnia—from the latest innovation in mattresses (so what is your "sleep number"?) to the newest prescription medication (and will you get addicted to it?), from herbal teas to mind-numbing late-night television. Perhaps you've tried some of these remedies.

The problem is, when you are troubled by life, nothing works very well. Except being honest with God.

The next time you find yourself in the midst of a sleepless night, writhing in bed while your mind churns through all the fears and frustrations that wear you out, spend some time meditating with the psalmist—who found himself, just like you, deeply troubled and searching for God's relief.

The more you yearn for insight, clarity, and answers, the more things seem senseless and crazy. You only have energy enough to sigh deeply, but without getting any fresh oxygen. Worry piles on top of worry. Crisis tries to outdo crisis. Questions gather like frothy slime in a corner of a stagnant pond.

You yearn for peace, for rest, for comfort. And your mind goes to work.

5 I consider the days of old, and remember the years of long ago.

6 I commune with my heart in the night; I meditate and search my spirit:

It didn't use to be this way, you tell yourself. You used to be strong and alive and confident in God. You used to have a youthful optimism about life that enabled you to conquer any setback, presumably in the strength of God. Your past mocks your present. You remember and ponder and search for how it used to be, and beg God to bring back that fresh naivete. It was so much easier then, wasn't it?

And now it seems God has left you alone.

7 "Will the Lord spurn forever, and never again be favorable?

8 Has his steadfast love ceased forever? Are his promises at an end for all time?

9 Has God forgotten to be gracious? Has he in anger shut up his compassion?" . . .

You know the answers to those questions. It may seem that God has cut off love, broken promises, forgotten grace, and thrown out compassion. But that can't be. It's impossible. That is not the kind of God you know.

It's possible that God is in this. Maybe God is doing something you are having trouble seeing for the tears in your eyes.

Instead of doubting God, ask yourself questions like these: Is God using this time to take me to the next step of faith, to build some maturity in my life? Does God want me to experience this so I can help others through such dark times? Does God want me to understand both the dark and the light, so I can appreciate the light all the more?

Despite the evidence of your circumstances, that sounds much more like the God you know.

11 I will call to mind the deeds of the LORD; I will remember your wonders of old.

12 I will meditate on all your work, and muse on your mighty deeds.

Instead of mulling over all the problems and pains and fears we're tangled up in, instead of thinking back on how great things used to be, let us remember who God is. When we're troubled, let us focus on God's ways, God's wonders, God's provisions for us over the years. Let us turn our thoughts inside out, downside up, and consider God as God is.

That will put things back into perspective before the dawn comes.

God, I confess that I can get caught up in chaotic self-pity and forget who you are and what you are up to. I burrow down into my fears and hurts, the slights and slanders, the confusion and crises, and lose all sight of you. Open my eyes to you, your work, and your calling on me. And give me rest so that I can begin again with the dawn.

Guided

Psalm 78

THEMES
Forgiveness
Care
Guidance
Skill
Redemption

¹ Give ear, O my people, to my teaching; incline your ears to the words of my mouth.

² I will open my mouth in a parable; I will utter dark sayings from of old,

³ things that we have heard and known, that our ancestors have told us.

⁴ We will not hide them from their children; we will tell to the coming generation the glorious deeds of the LORD and his might, and the wonders that he has done. . . .

The psalmist recounts for the people of Israel the story of their ancestry, their spiritual history—warts and all. In this lengthy song he lets it all out: the good, the bad, and the really awful.

Through it all he shows how God has miraculously worked. If you read the whole psalm you'll see lots of destruction, stubbornness, outright rebellion, and yet grace, compassion, and provision. It's all intended to educate the people about their past—and how they got to where they are now. Perhaps as a result, the psalmist certainly hoped, the people would learn from their past and follow God fully with heart, mind, and soul.

The psalmist ends his extensive historical journey with the example of King David, thereby reminding the people—and us today—of God's everlasting promises.

⁷⁰ He chose his servant David, and took him from the sheepfolds;

⁷¹ from tending the nursing ewes he brought him to be the shepherd of his people Jacob, of Israel, his inheritance.

⁷² With upright heart he tended them, and guided them with skillful hand.

That's a lovely, warm portrait of the shepherd boy who tenderly cared for the lambs under his responsibility, and who became the shepherd of the people of Israel. And he tended his nation with as much tenderness, skill, and righteousness as he did his flock of fluffy little lambs. It's a beautiful reminder of God's provision in the midst of so much negativity.

But, wait a minute . . . David?

He was the one who lusted after that woman next door in the bathtub, committing adultery. The one who had her husband put to death. The one who danced naked and unashamed before his victorious army, humiliating his wife. The one who ran away from conflict with a total lack of trust in God. The one who even pretended to be crazy to avoid being caught by enemy forces. He was the one who so frequently in the Bible seems weak and ignorant and deceptive and lustful, shirking God's wise guidance.

He was the one we've been getting to know through so many of these psalms, in which he cries out in loneliness, fear, and faithlessness, begs God for unwarranted forgiveness for his latest fraud, or pleads for the bloody destruction of his foes.

So is that the David the psalmist is describing here so rapturously?

Yes. Read the whole psalm and you'll see that David, just like Israel the people of God, is the subject of God's constant, abundant forgiveness.

Time after time David, as well as the nation as a whole, rebelled against God's guidance, rejecting, ignoring, running from God. And time after time God ultimately brought him back under God's wings of compassionate shelter.

God took this frail, faulty, fragile human being and guided and cared for him just as David had guided and cared for the lambs under his charge. And God can do that for you too.

That's something that we, "the coming generation," should keep in mind, and trust no matter how we fail.

God, these psalms are filled with human failure and faithlessness. And I can surely identify. They are also filled with your forgiveness, care, guidance, and unshakable love. I cannot escape from it. And despite the occasional appearances to the contrary, I don't want to. Guide me as you guided David.

Restored

Psalm 80

THEMES

Abandonment
Salvation
Acceptance
Redemption
Choices

¹ Give ear, O Shepherd of Israel, you who lead Joseph like a flock! You who are enthroned upon the cherubim, shine forth

² before Ephraim and Benjamin and Manasseh. Stir up your might, and come to save us!

³ Restore us, O God; let your face shine, that we may be saved. . . .

A friend of mine woke up one morning to find himself utterly lost. Oh, he knew where he was. He just didn't know how he got there.

Back in college, when I first knew him, he had a clear path in life. He had excellent job prospects in journalism, his major, a field he dearly loved. In fact, back then he used to say newspaper ink ran in his veins. There was one particular job opportunity he knew would totally fulfill his creative nature and provide a significant outlet for his gifts. But it involved a good bit of financial risk and would demand a lot of time, and if he didn't work hard at it the chances were good that it would all unravel. And yet, it seemed perfectly suited for him. His mind raced with the possibilities. And it all seemed fueled by the Spirit. It felt like God had made him for this.

The woman he was dating, and getting increasingly serious with, wasn't quite as enamored of the possibilities. She urged her father, who headed a well-regarded financial services firm, to consider making him a job offer. She told my friend that this would be good enough—good enough to provide for all their needs, good enough to get by. It would be safe. Against his gut feeling if not his better judgment, he went along with the plan.

I lost track of him after college, but years later reconnected with him online. I learned that my old friend had indeed married, started working at the family firm, and before long found himself miserable as he could be. And he could never forget the "what ifs."

It was too late, wasn't it? He could never make his wife understand, let alone his in-laws. He was imprisoned by the "good enough." He could never see his dreams, his lost possibilities, restored.

¹⁷ But let your hand be upon the one at your right hand, the one whom you made strong for yourself.

¹⁸ Then we will never turn back from you; give us life, and we will call on your name.

19 Restore us, O LORD God of hosts; let your face shine, that we may be saved.

My friend's tale is hardly unique. Because of our own stupid choices or the pressures of others upon us, many of us find ourselves in a place far away from our dreams, from the possibilities that once seemed to be God-given. And often that leads us to drift away from the God who fueled those dreams. We feel abandoned. Lost. Forgotten. Even though we're the ones who wandered away.

There comes a time to ask God to help us come home to ourselves. To give us life again. To look down on us and shine on us once again. There comes a time to ask God to hear our heartfelt prayer . . .

"Restore us, O LORD God of hosts." I want you back, God. I want me back. I want to be saved from this life of bad choices and no integrity. I want to be the person you made me to be. I want you to smile on me with pleasure and delight once again.

That's what my friend prayed. Will you join in the prayer as well? It may not change your circumstances, but it can change your attitude and restore your hope.

God, I know that my selfish choices, my fear of risk, my desire to protect myself, have resulted in some circumstances that may be keeping me from thriving. I know I may not be able to change those circumstances, certainly not easily, but I know that you can be with me in them. Shine your face upon me. And let me experience your restoration.

Satisfied

THEMES
Satisfaction
Hunger
Neediness
Fulfillment
Joy

10 I am the LORD your God, who brought you up out of the land of Egypt. Open your mouth wide and I will fill it. . . .

I was about thirty pounds overweight and feeling every ounce of it. I hadn't exercised regularly in a long, long time. That's not good. With the encouragement of a friend, I started jogging and working out, and even participated in the annual 10K road race that I had watched on the sidelines for years, assuming I could never, ever do such a thing. I began to eat smaller portions and much healthier meals—little to no salt, fresh seasonal vegetables, organics, all the good stuff.

Frankly, it took some adjusting. But before long, whenever my healthy friend would cook a meal, I could actually taste the food as it was supposed to taste. And instead of wolfing down whatever was on my plate, I could enjoy the smaller portions and feel completely satisfied. I even dropped those thirty pounds over several months.

This same approach—involving simplicity, healthfulness, balance, and enjoyment—can be applied to our spiritual life. After all, we live in a fast-food culture, one that infects much more than our physical diet; it impacts our life in full. We are surrounded by technology, information, culture—some of it healthy and pure, but much of it pure garbage. A diet like that can only cause our souls to become sick and bloated.

As a result, we become hungry for something real, something pure and holy within us. Something simple and clean and healthy. We yearn for the energizing presence of God within us.

And meanwhile, God is yearning to fulfill our hunger, to satisfy us with premium provisions:

16 I would feed you with the finest of the wheat, and with honey from the rock I would satisfy you.

So how do we experience healthy spiritual satisfaction?

We have to recognize that we are indeed hungry—that what we're getting from the world is only making us fat and unhappy.

We have to choose God's provisions instead, we have to seek them and work at finding them, realizing that we can only be truly satisfied by the good stuff.

We have to be able to hear and respond to God's generous offer to satisfy us. That means we have to be with God. Eat the body and blood of God's Son. And be satisfied.

Are you satisfied? Do you feel full of God's good spiritual provisions? Or do you need to change your diet?

God, I admit that I am taking in a lot of junk. Both physically and spiritually. It's no wonder I feel weak and aimless and fat and out of shape. Help me get healthy and active. Help me change my spiritual diet and get my priorities in good order. Fill me with your wholly satisfying spiritual nourishment. And let me thrive.

Nested

THEMES

Sanctuary

God's Presence

Holiness

Joy

Worship

1 How lovely is your dwelling place, O LORD of hosts!

2 My soul longs, indeed it faints for the courts of the LORD; my heart and my flesh sing for joy to the living God.

It seemed huge to me, like a cathedral, with a lovely heavenly themed painted ceiling. That's the way I remember the first church I recall being inside. I'm sure it's not all that large, maybe not as impressive as I remember it, but it made an impact on me. It was a Gothic stone Methodist church in Morgantown, West Virginia.

I had surely at that young age never been in any larger space than that. And people sang beautifully, and my father got up and said beautiful, reassuring, challenging words I didn't really understand. I just remember looking up at the ceiling and being amazed.

How many worship spaces have I found myself amazed in over the years since?

Everything from a tiny, white clapboard country church that oozed with plain piety to a soaring cathedral in Rio de Janeiro that literally took my breath away.

A Buddhist temple in Thailand covered with gold and precious stones and metals.

A Zen garden outside Iguazu Falls, Brazil, overlooking three nations.

A newly constructed and impossibly ornate and exquisite Hindu temple in the suburbs of Atlanta.

A small Catholic parish in the town square of a Costa Rican village, whose choir sang like angels, their anthem wafting and echoing around the valley like a dream.

Cathedrals and chapels and everything in between.

Each one of them, and so many more, home.

3 Even the sparrow finds a home, and the swallow a nest for herself, where she may lay her young, at your altars, O LORD of hosts, my King and my God.

4 Happy are those who live in your house, ever singing your praise.

God dwells in the unexpected as well as the expected places. Gorgeously constructed edifices that took centuries to complete, and tiny natural gardens offering a glimpse of creation.

And right where you are right now.

There is nothing more moving and joyful and wonderful than spending time in a holy space sanctified for the purpose of worshiping God. This same God dwells within you. So wherever you are, no matter what time of day it may be, you can focus your attention on the living God and, like the sparrow searching for a home, like the swallow building a nest for her family, you can be there.

Be there now.

God, I yearn to be in your presence. Bring me together with my family of faith to worship you in my corporate worship space. But let me not forget that your dwelling place is always within me as well. My heart and my flesh sing for joy to you.

Turned

Psalm 85

THEMES
Listening
Peace
Faithfulness
Direction

6 *Will you not revive us again, so that your people may rejoice in you?*

7 *Show us your steadfast love, O LORD, and grant us your salvation.*

8 *Let me hear what God the LORD will speak, for he will speak peace to his people, to his faithful, to those who turn to him in their hearts.*

When I was a kid, television sets usually came with extendable rabbit ear antennas. I remember the constant aggravation of moving the long chrome aerials this way and that in order to find the clearest picture possible. It could be an infinitely frustrating process and sometimes ended up with the TV set turned off. But, oh, the thrill when suddenly the picture popped in clearly.

It's amazing what we had to do in the "old days" in order to receive the signal we were searching for. With cable and satellite connections, we no longer need such a complicated method of seeking a signal.

Or do we? Not long ago, after realizing I was paying an awfully big bill for the cable television that I rarely ever watched, I decided to switch to over-the-air antenna reception and even bought a brand new set of rabbit ear antennas. But about the same time, by Congressional decree, the signals that local television stations sent over the airwaves switched from analog to digital, which meant my TV was no longer capable of receiving any signals without a digital converter box. Now, ironically, even with this new box on top of my television set, I am back to maneuvering rabbit ears in order to bring in the local stations.

Something occurred to me one day as I was moving the antennas around wildly searching for a signal that wouldn't give me a migraine: Sometimes I feel the same frustration with God. I'm not picking up God's signal. It seems all I'm receiving is static.

Even now I feel I'm at a point in my life where I am trying to listen for what's next. Which way should I turn? And will I be so busy trying to figure out which way to turn that I pay no attention to that still, small, whispering voice that speaks peace?

If only God would say something now, while we wait. Now, while we are quiet.

What do we do in that time of waiting? We look back at our past, see how we got to the point we are right now. We think again of how we hope and pray it will be. We want to be realistic, but we want to live wholly and fully in God's abiding presence.

So what do we do now? How do we wait? How do we listen?

Verse 8 reveals the key: *"[F]or he will speak peace to his people, to his faithful, to those who turn to him in their hearts."*

Instead of running around trying to find a direction for your life, turn to God in your heart. You know the direction to turn: To your faith community. Your scriptures. Your trusted mentors. Your prayerful meditation.

Right now, as you wait, as you listen, you have turned in one direction or another: to God, or to your past ways that haven't worked, when you ignored God and preferred to do what seemed best to you.

The psalmist reminds us that God will speak peace to those who faithfully turn their hearts toward God. That's the only way to gain a clear picture in life.

God, it's very noisy right now and it's hard to hear your voice. The static is filling my mind and I can't see very clearly. But I turn my heart to you. Let me live fully in the place where I am right now, the place of quiet, the place of waiting, the place of expecting you to speak to me.

Wholehearted

Psalm 86

THEMES
Devotion
Learning
Pursuing God
Thankfulness
Dedication

11 *Teach me your way, O LORD, that I may walk in your truth; give me an undivided heart to revere your name.*

12 *I give thanks to you, O LORD my God, with my whole heart, and I will glorify your name for ever.*

13 *For great is your steadfast love toward me; you have delivered my soul from the depths of Sheol.*

The *American Heritage Dictionary* defines the adjective "wholehearted" this way: "Marked by unconditional commitment, unstinting devotion, or unreserved enthusiasm."

That's what God wants of us. That's the way God teaches us to live, to honor God with "an undivided heart," to thank God "with my whole heart." No holding back. No reservations. No doubts. No distractions.

No way! Life isn't that easy, is it? There are far too many holes in our heart for us to be wholehearted followers of God.

Even with all God has given us, done for us, provided us with, we have far too many people, habits, hobbies, practices, jobs, tasks, and interests to distract us, to generate conditions to our commitment, and to deflate our devotion.

How do we get realistic about this?

First, let's not get too hard on ourselves about it. After all, we have tons of responsibilities in life, to our families, our job, our friends, our church duties, our civic responsibilities. Even to our own selves—our need for relaxation, stimulation, self-improvement, and fun.

But who says all those things can't be subsumed under our wholehearted commitment to God? It's all of a piece. It all simply flows out of a determination, a decision, a desire to be teachable, to walk with God, to open our hearts to God's love.

I had a conversation with a guy I knew through work over coffee once. He was moaning about the seemingly infinite duties he was trying to balance and juggle. On top of his regular job and family responsibilities, he'd volunteered in a leadership role with a drug and alcohol rehabilitation ministry in his community. Over the years he found his unpaid workload kept growing—he was supposed to train new volunteers, but that soon involved cultivating more volunteers, which involved helping with fundraising, which involved a lot of budgeting work . . . and on and on it went, like a wild snowball careering down a mountainside picking up all sorts of debris along the way. It was all about to crash. And he'd volunteered for it!

I commiserated with him and tried to be as sympathetic as I could be. But then, rather innocently, I asked him, "Well, why did you get into this in the first place?"

I was stunned when I saw tears well up in his eyes. I think he was just as stunned by it. He couldn't even speak for a few minutes, tried to take a sip of his coffee to gain some composure and nearly choked on it.

Finally, with some pain, he said, "My sister. You know, I can't believe I had almost forgotten. When she was in her late teens, she went through a rough time with a variety of addictions that eventually caused her death. We tried so hard to help her, but she ran from all of us. She ended up on the street, alone. After she died I promised God I would do whatever I could to make sure other people don't find themselves in the place where they have nothing and nobody and nowhere to go."

So this was God's calling on him. This was his way of wholeheartedly serving God, of sharing God's steadfast love with others.

As he spoke I could see his whole countenance shift. The sparkle came back in his eyes, and it wasn't the tears, it was the knowing. Knowing that God was blessing this work, as trying and tough as it could be at times. And knowing that it mattered.

What does God want your heart for? How will God love others through you—because you've given God your whole heart?

God, pull together all the pieces of my life into a whole that serves and honors and loves you undividedly, wholeheartedly, forever. Teach me your way, O Lord, that I may walk in your truth for me.

Refreshed

THEMES

Joy

Life

Refreshment

Reality

Connection

God's Presence

1 On the holy mount stands the city he founded;

2 the LORD loves the gates of Zion more than all the dwellings of Jacob.

3 Glorious things are spoken of you, O city of God. . . .

7 Singers and dancers alike say, "All my springs are in you."

You've experienced it, haven't you?

It can come when you look deeply into the eyes of someone you love and feel the connection that goes beyond mere physicality or emotion, but indeed is spiritual in every sense.

It can come when you stand at a magnificent waterfall, or on a peaceful beach pulsing with riotous waves.

It can come in the midst of a moving worship service, during a glorious anthem or perhaps in the Eucharist when the priest raises the bread and the wine given for all.

It can come when you feel the pleasure of God in your act of sacrificial service, or in your creative expression.

It can come in some totally unexpected time or place, but even so you know immediately what it is.

It's a fountain of refreshing clean water springing up in your innermost depths. It's the sense that something utterly genuine and real beyond reality is bubbling up within you, connecting you to the One who is all and in all. It's the effervescent certainty of God around and beyond you, the very presence of God within you.

The psalmist wrote of Jerusalem, calling it the city of God, in celebratory tones. But this city symbolizes the presence of God. As a believer, you live in the city of God wherever you are.

Remember what Jesus said to the Samaritan woman at the well—someone a good Jewish man would never speak to—after he asked her to give him a drink from the community water source in the heat of the day. Jesus said, *"If you knew the gift of God, and who it is that is saying to you, 'Give me a drink,' you would have asked him, and he would have given you living water. . . . [T]hose who drink of the water that I will give them will never be thirsty. The water that I will give will become in them a spring of water gushing up to eternal life"* (John 4:10, 14).

This is a brief psalm, so consider adding to it. How would you describe living in the city of God, in the very presence of the Almighty, wherever you are? What is it like to experience the springs within? Recall the many times you have experienced this sacred refreshment yourself. Even in the spiritually and emotionally thirsty times of life, there's a fountain of joy, hope, and life springing within you.

Perhaps right now you just don't feel it, but it's there. You know it's there. So join in the song, move with the dance, and praise God for filling you with the lively springs of eternity.

God, remind me of your living presence within me. I get so distracted. I become numb to the glorious fountain within my soul. But I am within you, and you are within me. I dwell in the city of God. Let me join in the celebration, the singing and the dancing, and let the springs of life and love overflow me and splash all around me.

Shunned

6 You have put me in the depths of the Pit, in the regions dark and deep.

7 Your wrath lies heavy upon me, and you overwhelm me with all your waves.

In his book *Soul Provider*, Edward Beck, a Passionist Roman Catholic priest, recounts an awkward encounter he had one weekend at a retreat center some years ago when he was leading a women's retreat. Tired from his travel and the first session, he was taking a bath in a bathroom he had been told he shared with another priest who was leading a different retreat that same weekend. Edward was relaxing in the warm bubbly water—until he heard someone in the next room. Suddenly a balding, bespectacled man burst in and, though surprised to find someone in the tub, calmly introduced himself. It was Henri Nouwen—one of the church's most eloquent writers and thinkers.

Despite Edward's obvious uneasiness, Henri chatted amiably and honestly with his fellow priest. He began sharing about a recent deeply hurtful experience. He felt wounded because he had bared his soul to someone he considered a close friend, but who couldn't take the honesty and, as a result, abandoned him. Henri told Edward how tough the resulting loneliness was for him. "When you get rejected by someone, it's hard to remember you're beloved," he said.

Before long, Nouwen rose from the stool he'd been sitting on and bid Edward a good night. They never had another chance to continue their conversation.21

8 You have caused my companions to shun me; you have made me a thing of horror to them. I am shut in so that I cannot escape;

9 my eye grows dim through sorrow. Every day I call on you, O Lord; I spread out my hands to you. . . .

18 You have caused friend and neighbor to shun me; my companions are in darkness.

I've read many of Nouwen's books and always found his freedom to reveal his loneliness and abandonment to be liberating, because I identified with those interior battles. Nouwen constantly pushes us toward utter authenticity in our relationship with God, with self, and with others—and yet he reveals the possible troubling consequences.

Some years ago after I had discovered Nouwen's books and began devouring them, I lost a close friend of many years after sharing some deeply personal feelings and fears with him. He too apparently couldn't handle it as he would no longer return phone calls or letters. He simply vanished.

Perhaps you can identify. Maybe you're feeling that dark, overwhelming emptiness of abandonment and loneliness, whether from a relationship broken, or from realizing you haven't yet even had a relationship in which you felt you could be utterly open and authentic.

The cry of the psalmist resonates deeply inside you. He is desperately wounded, shunned and alone. He sees no one to whom he can turn. Scholars note that this is the only one of the prayers for help in the book of Psalms that doesn't go on to express trust or thanks or praise in the midst of the darkness. It hurts that much.

It doesn't appear, even from reading Nouwen's later writings, that he ever fully made peace with his woundedness. That may be so for all of us. And yet, through it all, his lively faith was strong and intense. He lived the questions, he moved into the doubts, he stood against the fears.

When you find yourself in the depths of the pit, overwhelmed by abandonment and alone in the dark, search your heart for the reasons why. If you were wrong, try to make amends. If others simply weren't ready for your openness, accept the situation. Let this be a time when you too live the questions, move into the doubts, and stand against your fears.

God, in those times when it feels as though I have been abandoned by those I care about, and even by you, remind me that you are nevertheless there, and that you love me, and that you want me to live an honest and open life. Even though it may hurt me deeply at times to do so, I know there is no more fulfilling way to live. Help all of us who are wounded to reach out to one another rather than shunning, to love unhesitatingly rather than avoiding, and to accept others as you do, infinitely.

Counted

Psalm 90

THEMES
Life
Aging
Wisdom
Satisfaction
Fulfillment
Appreciation

1 Lord, you have been our dwelling place in all generations.

2 Before the mountains were brought forth, or ever you had formed the earth and the world, from everlasting to everlasting you are God. . . .

4 For a thousand years in your sight are like yesterday when it is past, or like a watch in the night. . . .

God is timeless. Never aging, never changing, God is the same yesterday, today, and tomorrow.

As for me, the older I get, the faster time flies. Yesterday I was twenty-five. Today I'm more than double that. And I realize I have less time remaining, certainly, than I've had so far.

You may not be where I am yet. Trust me, you will be tomorrow, or at least the day after. And the psalmist reminds both of us not to let ourselves be surprised by the passing of time, but to appreciate it, count it, revel in it, enjoy it, and above all live in it to the full.

When I was a kid, I thoroughly enjoyed science fiction stories that gave a hint of what life would be like in The Future. We'd scoot around in the sky in atomic-powered car-jets, or even better, jet packs right on our backs. Our homes would be filled with robotic conveniences, so that we'd wake up in the morning and our breakfast would be served automatically. Of course, peace would reign throughout the world—we just had pesky aliens to deal with. I can remember as a kid figuring out how old I would be when that magic and futuristic year 2000 arrived—and it sounded so old. Would I even still be alive?

Sometimes I feel disappointed that we have largely still not risen above gas-powered cars with rubber tires on roads. And yet the other day I had to laugh as I drank my coffee that made itself automatically just before I woke up, then programmed my combination washer/dryer unit to wait a few hours, then wash and dry and tumble my clothes until I got home from work, and meanwhile my robotic little vacuum cleaner was programmed to scoot around like a hockey puck on steroids for a couple of hours while I was out. Astonishing! I was living in the future I had dreamed of as a boy!

And that's not to mention the fact that I can bring the whole world into my home via cable television and the internet—futuristic dreams marveled over when I was just a kid and we could get only three channels on our massive family TV set. I can still recall when a new station started up—the local public broadcasting outlet. We'd sit around for hours watching programs about origami and yoga just because they were on this brand new channel.

> *10 The days of our life are seventy years, or perhaps eighty, if we are strong; even then their span is only toil and trouble; they are soon gone, and we fly away. . . .*
>
> *12 So teach us to count our days that we may gain a wise heart. . . .*

Time flies indeed, and before we know it, the future can become the past and our days are done. The psalmist reminds us to count our days, to treasure the time God gives us. Let's not fritter our life away with mundane distractions. Let's rather seek to discover and use our gifts for the common good, finding fulfillment in every moment God gives us.

> *14 Satisfy us in the morning with your steadfast love, so that we may rejoice and be glad all our days.*

That may be the key right there. To start out each morning realizing and appreciating God's steadfast love for us. Understanding that God is there, has always been there, will always be there, above it all, providing all we need for the most fantastically fulfilling life we could ever imagine.

Start your day with that reminder. Then strap on your jet pack and see where God takes you.

God, I don't want to waste a second. I want to live it. Remind me of my calling, my gifts, the resources and talents you've given me, so that I can live them today. Give me the wisdom I need to appreciate the time you give me, and may I spend it gladly to your glory.

Covered

THEMES
Fear
Terror
Safety
Security
Protection
Prayer
Trouble
Anxiety

¹ You who live in the shelter of the Most High, who abide in the shadow of the Almighty,

² will say to the LORD, "My refuge and my fortress; my God, in whom I trust." . . .

While on vacation, I had an unfortunate run-in with a henna tattoo artist on Rio's Ipanema Beach.

I had given in to a friend's encouragement to have a Celtic band drawn around my right bicep, assured it would disappear in a week or two. While my friend ran to the hotel to fetch some money, the young tattoo artist started to work diligently on the intricate design as I lay peacefully in the sun. After a few minutes three of his fellow tattoo artists sat down in the sand and began talking with him. They seemed a friendly bunch, though I couldn't understand their Portuguese and felt a little threatened since I was now alone. One guy offered to draw a tattoo on my right calf. I told him I wasn't interested. He assured me it was no problem. No, I insisted. But before I knew it, this guy started drawing a large sun on my calf. I told him to stop, I wasn't paying for it, but he laughed and kept drawing. I was afraid to move while the first man worked on my arm, and, well, maybe he was just being friendly after all.

After he finished, he asked in broken English for the money I now owed him—he wanted a hundred bucks! I said I owed him no money because I told him not to do it in the first place. He was not happy. After a few minutes of arguing, he and his cohorts took off, and then my friend returned with the money to pay for my arm tattoo.

Every day I was on the beach, the angry artist or one of his buddies would approach me and demand the payment. I stuck by my guns, probably foolishly. One day the guy apparently threatened me with death; after he stalked off an acquaintance nearby said he recognized the word "kill" in his mutterings to me. Consequently, I spent the rest of my time in Rio looking over my shoulder frequently, knowing the big sun tattoo on my right calf was a dead giveaway if any of his friends spotted me.

The last day I was on the busy beach, one of the tattoo artists demanded payment for his brother, but left after only a minute or two, seemingly having given up on the weeklong extortion attempt. A few minutes later as I began packing up my stuff, I discovered my shorts were missing with about twenty bucks and a watch in them. I guess he got paid.

His threats were a constant fear as I walked the streets of Ipanema that week with my friend, often in the dark of late evening. It's scary enough sometimes just walking in your own neighborhood after dark.

And that's not enough to fret about. What if your finances take a dive? Or you get sick at the worst possible time? Or you just have too much going on with school or work or all your other responsibilities piling on at once? Or something really bad happens to your best friend or family member?

Then add the news reports of terrorist attacks, natural disasters, violent crime, on and on and on. It's scary.

Yes, this can be a terrifying world. And that doesn't seem right; it's certainly not fun. You want to be hopeful and optimistic about the future. You want to live your life to the full, rather than cower under your bedcovers waiting for something bad to happen—as it most assuredly will.

So today, don't get sidetracked by anxiety. Let the voice of the psalmist sing into your mind and heart and soul. See yourself in the safe arms of God—covered by God's wings of strength and safety:

4 [H]e will cover you with his pinions, and under his wings you will find refuge; his faithfulness is a shield and buckler.

5 You will not fear the terror of the night, or the arrow that flies by day,

6 or the pestilence that stalks in darkness, or the destruction that wastes at noonday. . . .

Living under the shelter of God's wings—abiding in the shadow of the Almighty. That's not cowering under the covers or fearing who's following you on the strange city street; that's moving through the world and everything it has to throw at you surrounded by the spiritual protection of God. It's an awareness—deep down into your soul—that God loves you and is watching out for you. After all, God says:

14 Those who love me, I will deliver; I will protect those who know my name.

15 When they call to me, I will answer them; I will be with them in trouble, I will rescue them and honor them.

Do you see yourself in that safe place? God doesn't want you holed up in some bunker. God wants you out in the world shining the light. And that's all the more reason to call on God's protection and care.

Take a step out into the danger zone of your everyday world. See what happens in the power and protection of the Holy One.

I'll admit, God, that I can get very anxious at times. It seems that I live in a world that on its surface sometimes seems totally out of control. Help me trust that you are there, you are almighty, and you are holding me close to you in a very safe place. Give me the encouragement I need to go out there and be myself—with you.

Launched

Psalm 92

THEMES
Morning
Attitudes
Happiness
Praise

1 It is good to give thanks to the LORD, to sing praises to your name, O Most High;

2 to declare your steadfast love in the morning, and your faithfulness by night,

3 to the music of the lute and the harp, to the melody of the lyre.

There is that blessed but all-too-brief moment when you wake up in the morning—your mind slides out of slumber into wakefulness, and it's blissfully empty. All you know is that you're waking up in your warm bed and it's a new day.

And then your wits light up and your mind starts thinking about everything that's on your agenda for today. You get hit by the fear of how you're going to pay that bill, or the concern about your loved one who just received that bad medical diagnosis, or that major presentation you're supposed to prepare. And what about that funny sound your car started making, and that important phone call you forgot to return yesterday, and the fact your friend has still not returned your calls, and . . .

It's all downhill from there. Your brain churns, your heart hurts, your stomach tightens, and you have to get up and face it all.

Oh, if only we could stay in that little moment of peace, that tiny oasis of mindlessness.

But what if we consciously set our mind to respond to the alarm clock with a song of praise? Sure, it sounds a little silly, but what if we trained ourselves to recognize, first thing every day, the reality that's far bigger than all our petty worries and concerns? What if we join in with the psalmist's song:

4 For you, O LORD, have made me glad by your work; at the works of your hands I sing for joy.

Here's how to start your day: When the alarm sounds, or you drift out of sleep without it, before your brain kicks into gear take a deep breath and sing for joy. And mean it. Sometimes I sing a verse from another psalm to get my mind and heart around the reality that faces me: *"This is the day that the LORD has made; let us rejoice and be glad in it"* (Ps. 118:24). You can use another psalm or Scripture passage or even a hymn.

Let it remind you that God has made this day and it's waiting for you. God will be with you every moment of this day, comforting you, nudging you, reminding you, loving you, speaking to you, providing for you, working through you. Launching you into hope and beauty and joy and meaning and purpose. Propelling you into a day of being God's beloved child.

If you can begin the day with this attitude, then, when you face all those things you used to worry about in your waking moments, you'll have the strength and wisdom you need from the One who created you, the One who made this day. And you'll be glad in the midst of it all.

God, help me make this attitude adjustment today and every day, so I can gain a fresh perspective on the reality of this day. No matter what I face today, this is the day you made, and I will rejoice and be glad in it.

Celebrated

Psalm 95

THEMES
Worship
Praise
Joy
Celebration
Party

1 O come, let us sing to the LORD; let us make a joyful noise to the rock of our salvation! . . .

2 Let us come into his presence with thanksgiving; let us make a joyful noise to him with songs of praise!

I remember it as if it were yesterday, and the memory still moves me. I was in the church choir composed of first, second, and third graders, forced to go by caring parents but actually enjoying the experience from time to time. The choir directors were a husband and wife team who were deeply gifted and passionate about their work—which with a full slate of choirs for every age must have kept them very busy. The choir I belonged to at the time, given the tender age of its members, typically sang sweet little anthems in church once a month or so. But one Sunday the church had an all-choir presentation—including everyone from the preschool kids to the youth choir to the full adult choir, as well as a small but potent orchestra of strings and brass.

There were so many choir members that we more than filled the ample choir loft. Risers were erected around the raised pulpit and in the open area in front of the pews. We had all practiced a well-known hymn, "O God, Our Help in Ages Past," for several weeks as the grand finale featuring all the choirs—my memory pictures it as several hundred people, but I bet I'm exaggerating.

As we all moved into our spaces, Mr. McDowell stood on a tall, rickety stand to direct the entire assemblage, with Mrs. McDowell at the organ. Sunlight streamed through the intricate stained glass windows. Mr. McDowell enthusiastically launched into his direction (and did he really almost topple off his stand, as I vaguely recall?) and the instrumental introduction began. Then the adult choir started with the first verse. Different groupings of choirs sang the various verses, and then all the choirs and the orchestra performed the powerful final verse.

We raised the roof of that old Gothic downtown church.

As a child I was profoundly moved by that joyful noise of unfettered praise; in fact, for the next year or two—and occasionally even now—I would sing the hymn in my mind as I went to sleep.

Perhaps you've had a similar experience of voicing your praise to God in worship. Maybe you enjoy the musical worship in your church or even sing in a choir. You may be used to a praise band that gets a little raucous sometimes. Or maybe your worship tradition is not quite so noisy—perhaps you prefer quiet, contemplative spaces in which to praise and worship God.

Where and how you do it doesn't matter, really. What matters is what's in your heart when you're there. Are you joyful? Are you thankful? Are you naturally expressing your praise to God for all God is and does? Are you celebrating at full throttle the glory of God in your life?

The psalmist calls the people of God together to make a joyful noise in praise. And coming together to worship as a congregation of faith is a vital part of our spiritual life. But the celebration can also be internal. It can break out when you stop focusing on your problems and fears and start realizing that almighty God is the one who has made you and who lovingly shepherds you:

> 6 *O come, let us worship and bow down, let us kneel before the* LORD, *our Maker!*

> 7 *For he is our God, and we are the people of his pasture, and the sheep of his hand. O that today you would listen to his voice!*

Are you listening? Is your worshipful heart and mind open and receptive? Do you know who and where and why you are in the hands of God? Are you ready to make a joyful noise about it?

Let the celebration begin!

God, sometimes the world is so noisy and crazy I need the peace and quiet of your presence to get myself together. But I realize I can joyfully praise you in that place, as well as in a noisy celebration. The important thing is to praise you wherever I am with the music in my heart. And I can do that right now.

Judged

Psalm 98

THEMES
Judgment
Righteousness
Fairness
Anticipation

⁷ Let the sea roar, and all that fills it; the world and those who live in it.

⁸ Let the floods clap their hands; let the hills sing together for joy

⁹ at the presence of the LORD, for he is coming to judge the earth. He will judge the world with righteousness, and the peoples with equity.

Many Christians take these verses as a preview of the return of Christ, who is said in the New Testament to be coming back at the end of time to judge the earth, separating the sheep and the goats. I never quite understood Christ's Second Coming. I don't remember hearing much about it at all in the church I grew up in, though later, in my youthful spiritual wanderings when I became involved in a college fellowship that met weekly, I realized it was a major theme of more conservative churches and organizations. Watch many of the Christian programs on cable TV and you'll find out more about the end times than you ever thought possible.

In one of those campus meetings I first heard about the Rapture–the sudden, unexpected return of Christ, like a thief in the night, calling all believers up into the air and taking them directly and immediately to heaven. One evening after learning about all this my buddies walked around the campus doing "Rapture practice," leaping as high up as we could in the air. We were excited about the prospect, which could happen at any moment, though it's rather embarrassing to remember now.

I went on to a seminary that is well-known for its emphasis on end times theology and Christ's return to judge the earth. It became very clear to me that many Christians focus a great deal on this aspect of biblical study. Whole libraries of books parse obscure Scripture texts to find clues as to when and how it will all happen. In recent years wildly popular fictional accounts have filled even secular bookstore shelves and bestseller lists.

Over time, I began to wonder if this focus on the timeline of the last days actually sidetracks believers from the more significant and central messages of Christ's gospel–loving and serving others, especially the poor and needy. Shouldn't we concentrate more on what Jesus taught about how to live in this world rather than trying to figure out when and how we'll get to the next?

What I discovered in my own experience is that this focus on supposedly literal details about what would happen and who would be raptured made me very sure of myself. Certainly, I would be taken away to glory, and I quickly judged those who would not be. I was safe, because I knew what was coming, I thought. Others who didn't believe or behave properly were not so safe.

Be sure, the psalmist tells us, God is coming. Somehow, someway, God is coming to judge the earth, and that includes each one of us. And God comes again and again, in a variety of ways and times, to guide us and refine us.

And it's important to keep in mind that it's God who is to do the judging, not us. Thankfully, God will judge with righteousness and fairness.

The psalmist depicts all this as a joyful, positive thing. The whole world, the seas and hills, the world and all who live in it, will be exultant about God's judgment. Because it's right and true.

Scholars and teachers will argue until the end of time about the intricacies of God's coming. But let's keep focused on what we're supposed to be doing in the meantime. Living as authentic and righteous a life as we can, following the ways of God as best we can, treating others fairly and lovingly rather than judging them. And praising the God who is our presence, our power, our righteousness all the days of our lives.

Do that and you'll be ready for whatever happens.

God, I admit I get hung up on this judging business. I know I'm not supposed to do it, but so many people around me are more than happy to judge others and find them wanting. I want to leave the judgment in your righteous hands. I want to live life like I know I'm supposed to, with joy and freedom, and let you sort it all out in the end.

Refocused

THEMES

Perspective
Faithfulness
Love
Goodness
Praise
Gratitude
Priorities

1 Make a joyful noise to the LORD, all the earth.

2 Worship the LORD with gladness; come into his presence with singing.

There are times in life when responding to the psalmist's call here is natural. We can let go of our cares and concerns and enter into joyful praise and worship, singing effortlessly about our God.

Other times, not so much. We may be able to drag ourselves out of bed and to a worship service, but we hardly have a song on our lips.

When I was in seminary I learned a valuable lesson about this. For a year I served as a student assistant pastor at a small storefront United Church of Christ congregation in South Dallas. The pastor, nearing retirement age, was trying to hold this aging flock of a few dozen members together in the most meaningful way possible.

When I volunteered for this internship, I got a lot more than I expected. Seminary students were expected to serve in a church for at least thirteen weeks in order to gain some ministry experience in the real world. Many would take on one particular ministry or function for the prescribed time and be done with it, but I wanted to fully engage in the pastoral experience in order to help me determine God's call for me—whether I should follow in my father's footsteps as a pastor or pursue work in religious communications.

So this pastor took me under his wing and put me to work. I preached once a month, taught the junior high school kids (all three of them) weekly, attended church meetings, folded the newsletter, went on hospital visits with him, helped lead the Wednesday evening Bible study, even sat in on pre-marital counseling sessions. Whatever he did as a pastor, I was his shadow.

Before long, carrying a major seminary class load, working at several part-time jobs to support my family, and being so actively involved in the ministry of this church started to take a toll on me. I began to feel taken advantage of by this pastor, even though I had volunteered for it all.

Then, after nearly a year of all this, my son was born. That blessed event consumed several busy days, making sure he and his mother were healthy, bringing him home to our duplex, helping out with feeding and diaper changes at all hours, and all that. In the midst of it all, I was supposed to preach that Sunday morning. I called the pastor the Friday before and told him how exhausted I was, and that I needed to skip this Sunday.

He sighed deeply. "Pete," he said very seriously, and rather unsympathetically I thought, "when you're the pastor of a church, you don't get to skip a Sunday like that. No matter what's going on in your life, no matter how rotten or tired you feel, your people need you to be there and lead them in worship."

I was stunned and upset, but too fatigued to argue, so I showed up that Sunday and preached. I have no idea now what I said.

Later I realized that this pastor himself was constantly dealing with personal issues, health problems, all manner of burdens, but he always showed up at church with a warm smile, a ready hug, and a word of encouragement.

Sometimes you just have to show up and go through the motions of worship. You just have to be there to hear with weary ears what the psalmist reminds us:

3 Know that the LORD is God. It is he that made us, and we are his; we are his people, and the sheep of his pasture.

4 Enter his gates with thanksgiving, and his courts with praise. Give thanks to him, bless his name.

5 For the LORD is good; his steadfast love endures forever, and his faithfulness to all generations.

When I don't feel like making a joyful noise, that's when I need to let the truths of this ancient song sink in. To let this psalm, no doubt sung beautifully and joyfully and loudly in the temple so many centuries ago, echo ever so lightly within my heart. To hear it. To know it. To let it shape my perspective, and reshape my priorities.

Gradually, over time, going through the motions enables us to stretch our spiritual muscles and helps us overcome our sadness, exhaustion, or self-centeredness.

Whatever is going on in our lives, God is worthy of worship. And in the grand scheme of things, ultimately, God's steadfast love and faithfulness will shine, banishing every shadow of darkness, every hint of pain and exhaustion forever.

So be there now. Enter into God's presence with thanksgiving and praise. Whatever it takes, give thanks. Praise God's name. Maybe it won't feel very authentic right now, but it will in time.

God, my bones hurt right now, my heart feels like a shattered piece of pottery. It's not easy to read this psalm, let alone mean it, let alone put it into practice and sing your praises. But accept the broken, shallow, nearly empty praises I can utter, and use them to rebuild my heart, to trust your wisdom, to sense and to share your love even when it seems impossible to do. I yearn to make a joyful noise to you. May it be soon.

Integrated

THEMES

Integrity
Honesty
Authenticity
Deception
Arrogance
Judgment

2 I will study the way that is blameless. When shall I attain it? I will walk with integrity of heart within my house;

3 I will not set before my eyes anything that is base. I hate the work of those who fall away; it shall not cling to me.

4 Perverseness of heart shall be far from me; I will know nothing of evil.

5 One who secretly slanders a neighbor I will destroy. A haughty look and an arrogant heart I will not tolerate. . . .

7 No one who practices deceit shall remain in my house; no one who utters lies shall continue in my presence.

8 Morning by morning I will destroy all the wicked in the land, cutting off all evildoers from the city of the LORD.

This sounds pretty harsh to our ears. We expect people to be more tolerant. It's hard not to react with revulsion to the psalmist's declaration to God that he will "destroy" those who slander others, that he won't tolerate arrogance, that he will banish liars and destroy all the wicked in the land.

So what does this psalm reveal about what God wants of us? It's rather clear when you strip away the bravado here:

First, God wants us to live lives of integrity. And second, God wants us to be careful about the people we surround ourselves with in life, because they can negatively impact our integrity.

Throughout history, leading individuals—whether clergy, politicians, business leaders, or other influential sorts—have been exposed as frauds, liars, double-minded deceivers. Often these self-righteous leaders of church and state demand particular values in society, thereby relegating large numbers of people to the margins, but then they are caught in some horrendous scandal that shatters all their credibility because of their hypocrisy. There was the conservative evangelical preacher who was outspoken in his opposition to homosexuality, until it was revealed that he frequently paid a hustler for sex. Or the conservative congressman, a staunch supporter of "family values," who was found propositioning young male pages via the internet. Time after time, such people who have no integrity but rather are consumed by hypocrisy are unmasked. And we seem to be shocked every time, but not really.

Frankly, I'm a little amused—but also angered—by people like that. (And I can understand the psalmist's resolution to kick them out of his house!) If they had walked in integrity in the first place, perhaps they could have come to terms with their own situation in healthy ways, and in turn helped others to do so as well.

God wants us to be integrated. God wants us to be ourselves, who God created us to be. God wants us to be honest—with God, with others, and perhaps most painfully, with ourselves. God wants us to walk with integrity, without deceit, without arrogance, but with a healthy understanding and acceptance of our humanness. And not only ours, but everyone else's.

Living a life of integrity may take some major restructuring of our situation, our relationships, or our responsibilities. It may mean taking ourselves out of the particular clique at school that arrogantly looks down on students of different races, religions, or orientations. Or speaking up when a work colleague cracks a demeaning remark about someone. It may mean reconsidering the websites we read, the leaders we pay attention to, even the company we work for or the church we attend. It may mean taking ourselves out of a relationship that is keeping us from being honest.

If we're experiencing a disconnect between who we are deep within—our God-given self—and associations such as these, the psalmist's message is clear: Walk with integrity. And that really is possible only when we are careful and intentional about what we let influence us: the people, the programs, the habits, the hobbies, the media, the environment, whatever it is.

It also takes time. And acceptance. And forgiveness. And reality.

Read verse 2 again. Living a life of blameless integrity takes study and contemplation, weighing options, digging deeply within ourselves, opening ourselves up to holy scrutiny, being accountable.

"When shall I attain it?" Good question.

Keep yourself busy working on that, and you won't have to worry about anyone else's failings.

God, I find it so easy to get sidetracked taking other people down when they fail to live lives of integrity. It makes me feel better about my own lack of authenticity. Help me to focus on my own blamelessness instead. There's plenty to work on. And it's risky. And scary. But I know you are calling me to "walk with integrity of heart"—so help me take the first steps.

Withered

Psalm 102

THEMES
Devastation
Exhaustion
Pain
Trust
God's Help

¹ Hear my prayer, O LORD; let my cry come to you.

² Do not hide your face from me in the day of my distress. Incline your ear to me; answer me speedily in the day when I call.

³ For my days pass away like smoke, and my bones burn like a furnace.

⁴ My heart is stricken and withered like grass; I am too wasted to eat my bread.

⁵ Because of my loud groaning my bones cling to my skin. . . .

⁷ I lie awake; I am like a lonely bird on the housetop.

I think it's the earliest memory of my life, when I was just a toddler. As it's imprinted on my brain, I was lying in my crib, looking out the window of my bedroom, probably having just awakened from a nap. I could see the neighbor's roof through this upstairs window. And in the gutter was a dark-hued baby bird, its head thrusting upward, its beak wide open. Alone. Waiting for its mother to come feed it.

If that image doesn't capture the helpless need the psalmist expresses here, I don't know what will.

In this psalm, the writer begs God to hear his heart's cry. It seems as though God is hidden away, silent, leaving the psalmist alone to wait like that hungry bird on the housetop. Personal devastation has laid waste to the psalmist's soul like a dry, hot drought lays waste to crops in wide ruined fields. Time passes inexorably, like smoke slowly wafting in the hushed air, without the aid of any refreshing breeze—it just hangs there, heavy and full, keeping him trapped in the haze of doubt.

You too have been through the scorching drought of the spirit. If you haven't, trust me, you will. It will put you in its lethargic spell, withering your heart like burnt grass at the height of the autumn equinox. Like the psalmist, you are hardly able to eat, sleep, or move. Doubt and acedia ravage you with a fire that seems to consume your very bones.

When life takes you there, you are left waiting for some sprinkle of rain, a breath of fresh air, some shred of hope. That's where the psalmist was. And, once again, he reminds himself, and us, that God is there as well. And at some point, God will "rise up and have compassion" (v. 13). "It is time," the psalmist prays, "the appointed time has come."

Wherever you are right now, let that sink in. God did it then. You know God has done it before in your life. And God will do it again. God will hear and work and act—perhaps in ways you don't expect or maybe even desire—but even so, God will act.

That toddler memory of mine? It doesn't end with the lonely baby bird on the rooftop. Mama swooped in with a juicy, writhing worm. As I watched through young eyes, I didn't know what was happening then. I do now.

God, my soul is withered by this situation in my life right now, and I know, at some level in my consciousness, that you are there, you know what's going on, and you know how desperately I want to be freed from this place. Remind me that you are indeed faithful. You are working in the midst of my devastation and exhaustion. You are bringing me all I need to get through this. Let me trust in that. And wait for you.

Freed

THEMES
Sin
Forgiveness
Freedom
Youth
Mistakes

1 Bless the LORD, O my soul, and all that is within me, bless his holy name.

2 Bless the LORD, O my soul, and do not forget all his benefits—

3 who forgives all your iniquity, who heals all your diseases,

4 who redeems your life from the Pit, who crowns you with steadfast love and mercy,

5 who satisfies you with good as long as you live so that your youth is renewed like the eagle's. . . .

Recently I watched a French film that got stuck in my brain. Frankly, despite the breathtaking scenery of Provence that makes the film a delight to watch, the surly attitudes and selfish behaviors of a couple of the main characters were so frustrating that I hardly felt any sympathy for them. It was frustrating to watch these damaged people try so hard to avoid relating positively to each other. Even so, I found myself thinking about it over the next few days.

The Grocer's Son is about a young man, Antoine, who had left his rural home years earlier to live a liberated life in the big city. It isn't very fulfilling, though, as he aimlessly moves from job to menial job and never truly finds any sort of meaningful relationship. Still, he is proudly independent—until his estranged father suffers a heart attack, and he is pressed to return home to Provence and help out. While his mother runs the family grocery store, he must drive his father's mobile grocery van to sell produce and sundries to mostly older inhabitants of the countryside. With virtually no patience for the slower pace of life in the country—and its frequently eccentric residents—Antoine can hardly conceal his loathing for the work. He is rude and sullen with his father's loyal patrons, and has no interest in the family work.

As unlikable as Antoine can be, his father seems to share a very similar personality. His furious disappointment in his son is palpable. We realize the two had had a major clash or two in the past leading to their estrangement—which is why Antoine can hardly tolerate having to help his ailing father.

But with the positive influence of a charming friend from the city—of course, she and Antoine fall in love—he slowly comes to the realization that, with a change in attitude, an acceptance of reality, and perhaps most of all the giving and receiving of forgiveness, he can actually warm to his fate and experience some measure of fulfillment, even in the boondocks of Provence.

The shift in attitude is so slow it's almost imperceptible—it has happened before you realize it. There's no climactic forgiveness scene, no teary confessions, hearty hugs, and pledges of love. The change of heart is subtle but no less real for it.

As one reviewer suggests, it really is a French variation of Jesus' prodigal son parable (Luke 15:11–32).[22] That is why the picture stuck with me. In fact, I realized that this is probably a truer depiction of the impact of forgiveness on our lives than some more dramatic one. It is life with all its subtle shades, moving in the direction of redemption and fulfillment and never quite fully arriving there, but certainly enjoying the environs of it. And even so, it's still reason to bless the Lord, to praise God with all that is within you.

Whatever it involves, whatever estrangement is in your past, God forgives all your iniquity. God heals and redeems you, crowns you with steadfast love and mercy. God satisfies you. And you are set free to praise God for all that. The psalmist reiterates this reality beautifully:

> *10 [God] does not deal with us according to our sins, nor repay us according to our iniquities.*
>
> *11 For as the heavens are high above the earth, so great is his steadfast love toward those who fear him;*
>
> *12 as far as the east is from the west, so far he removes our transgressions from us.*

Read that last verse again. Do you get it? If it said our sins were removed from us "as far as the north is from the south," that wouldn't mean a whole lot, because if you keep going north on the globe, you eventually will start heading south. But when you head east on the globe, and keep heading east, you never end up heading west. The distance is infinite. That's how far God has removed our transgressions, our mistakes, our sins, our failures from us.

You are forgiven. God will not deal with you on the basis of your mistakes and failures. You are free to begin living life without that baggage, without that fear and shame. This is a new day. And when you realize that, you can find fulfillment wherever you go, whatever you do.

God, I want so badly to believe this is true—that you have forgiven me. That I am clean and free and able to begin this day wholly yours. Crack open my heart just a bit today and let some of that light in. So that I can in turn share it with someone else.

Welcomed

Psalm 104

THEMES
Creation
Humanity
Diversity
Welcome
Acceptance

12 By the streams the birds of the air have their habitation; they sing among the branches.

13 From your lofty abode you water the mountains; the earth is satisfied with the fruit of your work.

14 You cause the grass to grow for the cattle, and plants for people to use, to bring forth food from the earth,

15 and wine to gladden the human heart, oil to make the face shine, and bread to strengthen the human heart. . . .

One of my favorite things to do is to take a walk or a run or a jog through Piedmont Park, the major community park in Atlanta. It's often called the "Central Park of Atlanta," and though the original in Manhattan dwarfs our little park here in the South, parts of Piedmont Park were designed by the sons of Frederick Law Olmsted, the noted landscape architect who laid out Central Park.

Piedmont Park contains a lake, an "active oval" for softball, soccer, and even volleyball, a wide lawn for concerts and events, a couple of playgrounds, tennis courts, and lots of leafy paths to meander. Which I do as often as I can.

One glorious autumn afternoon I walked through the park listening on my iPod to a thirty-minute musical loop by Tim DeLaughter called "Acceptance," which seemed fitting. While I inhaled the crisp smoky air and let the music soothe my thoughts, I started paying attention to the people all around me. What hit me as I opened my eyes to my environment there in the park was the rich diversity of the population at any given moment.

Anywhere I looked I found something different. There on the wide green were young men vigorously playing touch football. Dogs of all breeds and mixtures were walking their owners, often in talkative clusters. A father with an infant strapped to his chest pointed his toddler daughter to see the geese landing as though on skis on the lake surface. Groups of students from the nearby high school wandered aimlessly, talking and texting and laughing together. A large and animated family of several generations gathered around picnic tables sharing a splendid barbecued meal. An older couple walked arm in arm admiring the brilliant foliage and sharing the moment with each other. A homeless man with a well-worn backpack sunned himself on a park bench with a plaque that announced its donation by a late society matron.

There were people of all ages and sizes and shapes. Runners, walkers, strollers. Blacks, whites, Latinos, Asians, straights, gays, athletes and the out-of-shape. And all found a welcome home in the park.

The picture surrounding me was so beautiful in that moment that tears came to my eyes. Tears of joy and hope. This was the family of humanity, gathered here in the midst of God's creation.

This image occurred to me as I read Psalm 104—a song of praise to our Creator God for all the incredible beauty and diversity of this world and the whole created order, a psalm drenched with what Walter Brueggemann has called God's "exuberant generosity."[23] As you read these verses, open yourself up to read between the lines a bit:

> 24 *O LORD, how manifold are your works! In wisdom you have made them all; the earth is full of your creatures.* . . .
>
> 27 *These all look to you to give them their food in due season;*
>
> 28 *when you give to them, they gather it up; when you open your hand, they are filled with good things.* . . .
>
> 30 *When you send forth your spirit, they are created; and you renew the face of the ground.*

God's whole creation is marked by manifold diversity, and in wisdom God made them all. All—all people no matter who we are, all living creatures—look to God to provide their needs. All of us depend on God to fill us with good things. And so we are all in this together. We live in the created order marked by uniqueness and individuality, yet we live together under the glory of God.

Can we welcome one another in this place? Can we live together and enjoy the differences each of us brings?

In a *Day1* sermon, Jimmy Moor, who pastors a church near the park, drew an important lesson from this image: "It doesn't matter who you are, what your job is, how you are dressed, or what you've done. There's a place for you at Piedmont Park. The park comes to my mind sometimes when I think of what the church looks like at its best—a community where everyone is welcome and has the opportunity for healing and renewal."[24]

Is that the case in your congregation, your faith community? Is it a place of generous welcome for all, offering healing and renewal to whoever comes? What can you do to help make it so?

God, you created this world, this existence, for all of us who are part of it. Why do we avoid the other so intently? Help me to open my eyes and my heart to all around me, and welcome them in the spirit of love and fellowship that you extend to all of us. Help me make my congregation one marked by extravagant welcome and exuberant generosity to all.

Encouraged

THEMES
Thankfulness
Praise
Strength
God's Presence
Trust

Think back over the ways God has been at work in your life. The often painful growing edges of your soul. The experiences that taught you something important about life and how to live it. The surprise victories you can't explain without God. The ways you've overcome those constant temptations to be something other than who you are in order to be accepted or successful in the eyes of people who just don't get it.

Think about those times in your experience, and be encouraged. God has performed wonders among the people of God—and that includes you. God's deeds are worth remembering, celebrating, and sharing. Psalm 105 can help you put words to your worship of the God who has been so faithful in the past—though we tend to forget—and whom we can trust to encourage us in the present and the future.

1 O give thanks to the LORD, call on his name, make known his deeds among the peoples.

Remember when you struggled with confusion about the path your life was to take, overwhelmed by the conflicting options you faced? Or maybe there seemed to be no viable option for your future at all. What would bring you the most fulfillment? What were you made for? And how could you get there? But somehow God opened the door and you moved forward through it. And now here you are. Think back, give thanks, and tell somebody what God has done.

2 Sing to him, sing praises to him; tell of all his wonderful works.

Remember that time you really messed up in your close relationship? Out of selfishness or stupidity you did something you regretted, found yourself, out of fear or pride, spinning a web of lies, and only got more defensive about it as the pressure built. But in some way, God opened your eyes to what you were doing, melted your self-protection, and enabled you to come clean and begin to repair the damage you'd inflicted. God restored the relationship. Think back, give thanks, and tell somebody what God has done.

3 Glory in his holy name; let the hearts of those who seek the LORD rejoice.

Remember that period of your life when you drifted away from God, when you felt you could figure things out on your own, and you really didn't have time to be involved in religion? You enjoyed exploring life without this apparent crutch, for a time. But slowly, subtly, you began to miss some things—the sense of peace you experienced in quiet prayer, the joy of singing together in a worship service, the fulfillment of serving someone in need in God's name. You missed the challenge of wrestling with God's call on you to bring peace and meaning in the world, of figuring out what that meant each day in concrete expressions. You missed the stimulating and sometimes exasperating fellowship with other seekers who wanted, like you, to experience the best that God offers in life. And somehow, you found yourself back home in God's presence, rejoicing. Think back, give thanks, and tell somebody what God has done.

4 Seek the LORD and his strength; seek his presence continually.

Remember the time your heart was broken, your soul wounded by the loss of someone you treasured? You couldn't imagine life without the wisdom, the liveliness, the very presence of this person, but suddenly this person was gone. In grief you felt utterly alone and abandoned. But somehow you were able to wait for God in this time. In your weakness you longed for God's restoring presence, and you reached out to draw on God's strength. You began to understand that it takes intentionality and purpose and mindfulness and awareness to stay connected with God through this empty time— or in any time of life. You found God was there, waiting for you continually. Think back, give thanks, and tell somebody what God has done.

5 Remember the wonderful works he has done, his miracles, and the judgments he has uttered.

The next time life throws you a curveball, or you can't see the way ahead, or you face a down time, or you don't understand what's happening, remember. Think back. Recall the amazing things God has done for you and through you. Meditate on who God is, how God has taught you, what God has spoken to you in times past. It may be dark and silent for a while, but your trust in God is sure, and you'll be singing again before you know it. Because when you put things into perspective, seeing God's hand in whatever comes your way, and in the internal urges that get you moving and serving and loving, you can't help but be encouraged.

Give thanks . . . sing . . . glory . . . seek . . . remember. And stay connected in the presence of your awesome God.

God, it's easy for me to forget. To take for granted. To give up. To disbelieve. To keep the good stuff to myself. And it's no wonder I end up lost and weak. Thank you for the encouragement of the psalmist to call on you, to remember you, to seek you, to praise you, to brag about you. Make those actions as natural to me as breathing.

Stressed

THEMES
Anxiety
Distress
Stress
Peace
Deliverance

1 O give thanks to the LORD, for he is good; for his steadfast love endures forever.

2 Let the redeemed of the LORD say so, those he redeemed from trouble

3 and gathered in from the lands, from the east and from the west, from the north and from the south.

When you think of intensely stressful situations one might need to be redeemed from, a desert war zone would come quickly to mind. But sometimes, anxiety and distress can seem more intense to us in locations and situations that otherwise are quite normal and everyday.

Freelance photojournalist Ken Paprocki was on assignment in Afghanistan during the height of the early conflict there. Several times he found himself in the middle of rocket attacks. He accompanied night patrols in extremely dangerous areas where insurgents were known to be active. It was a life of unexpected roadblocks, unknown environments and cultures, unrelieved anxiety about what might happen next.

But what really surprised him was the level of stress he experienced after he returned home to the States. "It was like going from a camel's lope to riding a rocket. I felt fear in Afghanistan, but I was rarely worried. My only preoccupation was getting my shot and finding an Internet connection to send it off. But in New York, life is so utterly complicated that we are drowning in our daily regimen of tasks: networking, drumming up business, helping friends with meltdowns, dealing with family problems, having to shoehorn fitness into the day, having to call tech support just to watch a DVD."[25]

I'm sure you can relate to the level of distress he's talking about—whether you've been to Afghanistan or not. We may think it's a modern phenomenon, but it's not. The Israelites experienced soul-fainting distress thousands of years ago in a desert not far from where Paprocki was assigned.

4 Some wandered in desert wastes, finding no way to an inhabited town;

5 hungry and thirsty, their soul fainted within them.

6 Then they cried to the LORD in their trouble, and he delivered them from their distress;

7 he led them by a straight way, until they reached an inhabited town. . . .

Their lives had been turned upside down as they wandered, desperate for food and water, agonized by their plight. But God heard them and delivered them to safety.

35 He turns a desert into pools of water, a parched land into springs of water.

36 And there he lets the hungry live, and they establish a town to live in;
37 they sow fields, and plant vineyards, and get a fruitful yield. . . .

That's a beautiful word picture of a life provisioned by the generous mercies of God. Take it literally, take it figuratively, it's possible only with God's deliverance from the stressful and distressing circumstances of life–wherever we may be.

39 When they are diminished and brought low through oppression, trouble, and sorrow, . . .

41 . . . he raises up the needy out of distress, and makes their families like flocks.

42 The upright see it and are glad; and all wickedness stops its mouth.

43 Let those who are wise give heed to these things, and consider the steadfast love of the LORD.

Paprocki found ways to cope with the many distresses in the desert of modern life. Around his busy career he practices yoga, exercises, does whatever it takes to gain a measure of peace before the stress hits again. "I accept that worry's part of the price of living an exciting, interesting life."26

That's what we want, right? An exciting and interesting life? There is a price to pay for that in the form of some level of stress and anxiety. But know that there is a God whose "steadfast love endures forever." A God who stands ready to hear your cry for relief, for healing, and for peace in the midst of it all. A God who is ready to deliver.

God, sometimes my stress levels are overwhelming. I know there are some things I can do to take better care of myself–physically, mentally, and emotionally. But I come to you for the very important spiritual part of that care. More than anything I want an exciting and interesting life of love and service for you. Enable me, wherever I am today, to experience that to the full in the peace and care of your love.

Infuriated

THEMES

Anger
Attack
Justice
Punishment
Revenge

1 Do not be silent, O God of my praise.

2 For wicked and deceitful mouths are opened against me, speaking against me with lying tongues.

3 They beset me with words of hate, and attack me without cause.

4 In return for my love they accuse me, even while I make prayer for them.

5 So they reward me evil for good, and hatred for my love. . . .

The psalmist is really upset. Fiercely angry with his enemies. Thirsting for vengeance. And the verses following these contain some of the most harsh and vicious language in the Bible. Read them if you don't believe me.

So what do we do with this psalm, and so many others like it? For one thing, we can certainly identify with them. Over the years I have expressed very similar sentiments when attacked unfairly, only not in such flowery language.

How could that person I've known for so long, who I thought was a friend, treat me so hurtfully?

How could that search committee choose that other person instead of me for that job I really wanted, since I clearly had more experience?

How could the company, which I work for, so callously treat its workers, forcing us in the face of financial straits to do more work for less pay while its chief executives continue to enjoy huge salaries?

How could those new neighbors of mine be so incredibly noisy and rude and treat my property as though it were their trash dump?

How could that group of terrorists coldheartedly kill so many people to advance their brutal ideology?

God, they deserve your fierce judgment. Make them pay. Make them suffer!

Sound familiar to you?

So here are these angry, vicious words captured within the holy word of God. Some translations even try to soften the blow here by adding words in verse 6 to make it appear that the verbal attacks are really coming from the psalmist's enemies rather than from the psalmist himself. But that's an obvious cover-up.

Let's be honest: The psalmist had strong feelings. And so do we at times. And it must be OK to express them, even write them down for all posterity to shudder over and even be shocked by.

But in the end, we must leave those who attack us to God, who will sort it all out with absolute wisdom, love, and justice. We must trust that same God even in the midst of our stewing anger, and join with the psalmist who, perhaps begrudgingly, concluded:

30 With my mouth I will give great thanks to the LORD; I will praise him in the midst of the throng.

31 For he stands at the right hand of the needy, to save them from those who would condemn them to death.

It's natural to vent our rage, anger, and utter frustration when we're attacked. Go ahead, God can take it. Let yourself be totally honest with God about how you feel in the moment. You may feel some relief once you get it off your chest, and that can be what you need to do to put it in God's hands. Because, remember, judgment belongs to God. Justice is at the core of God's heart, and God will make all things right.

God is very clear throughout the rest of the Bible about what we're supposed to do instead: Not pay back. Not punish. Not argue against. Not fight. Instead, we're to be peacemakers. Lovers. Givers. We're to trust God to work out God's will in whatever way seems best to God. We're to shine God's light on our world. And we're to leave the people who drive us nuts with frustration and anger in God's hands.

Let it out. Express yourself. But keep it between you and your wise and just God, who stands with you in your pain.

God, in that moment of white-hot anger, when I am filled with fierce fury against others who I feel deserve no mercy, when I crave revenge with every cell of my hurting body, give me pause to breathe. To praise you. To give thanks to you in the midst of it all. And to trust you to bring about justice ultimately. And let me do my part to bring a little peace and light into the world today.

Wised Up

Psalm 111

THEMES
Fear
Wisdom
Praise
Community
Congregation
Faith

¹ Praise the LORD! I will give thanks to the LORD with my whole heart, in the company of the upright, in the congregation.

² Great are the works of the LORD, studied by all who delight in them.

³ Full of honor and majesty is his work, and his righteousness endures forever.

⁴ He has gained renown by his wonderful deeds; the LORD is gracious and merciful.

⁵ He provides food for those who fear him; . . .

Fear? God? I was doing great reading this psalm until that little word tripped me up. I don't like to be afraid. I bet I'm not alone.

Fear gnaws at your gut and your heart when you're not sure what's going to happen, and any alternative seems dreadful.

As a parent and grandparent, fear of the unknown seems to be my constant companion: Will they be safe? Will they be healthy? Will they live full lives? Will they truly find themselves? Will they love God? Those questions hang, consciously or not, in the spaces of my heart.

And for myself: Can I make it financially, especially in this economy? Will I do a good enough job to satisfy my employer, and myself? Will I face some horrendous health crisis or accident? Will the person I love most leave me? Will God approve of me?

There is plenty in life to engender fear. And I don't like it. That's one reason I want to be connected to God, to experience God's freedom and peace.

And then I read this:

¹⁰ The fear of the LORD is the beginning of wisdom; all those who practice it have a good understanding. His praise endures forever.

Well, I'd like to have wisdom for living. But it starts with fear, right?

The problem is, we misunderstand this kind of fear. This isn't a cowering, frantic, wide-eyed fright. This is humble respect, a deep and thorough acknowledgment of the place of God in the world and in my life. This fear is based on utter trust and a desire to follow God's way in every area of life.

When you start in that place, wisdom begins to flow. You see things in perspective. And the fears we catalogued at first—the fears of the unknown—fade away in the presence of the fear of the Lord.

And notice this: The fear of God takes practice. We have to continually learn and work at this proper approach to understanding God. Which means God knows we'll get it wrong. We'll take our eyes off God and onto the fearful things of the world and of life. But we must keep practicing.

And notice this too: The fear of God is not meant to be undertaken alone. The psalmist emphasizes that truth when he says "all those who practice it." In fact, the whole psalm has a community context. Reread the first verse and you'll see the praise of God comes out of the congregation, the "company of the upright."

It's difficult and perhaps even scares us a little to approach God alone. When we realize who God is and catch a glimpse of the power and authority God possesses, then, yes, that fear might get turned in the wrong direction. But joining together to come before God, praising the Lord together, learning God's ways as a community, expressing together God's love in action to a world in need–that's how wisdom is generated in our lives.

It begins with fearing God together. And the praise of God will endure forever.

God, I'll admit that the fears of my life occasionally–often–overwhelm my proper fear of you. Help me to come to the right starting point, with my brothers and sisters in the community of faith. And let me understand that that's just the beginning. I can't wait to see where it goes from there.

Raised

THEMES
Praise
Care
Distance
Understanding
Fulfillment

3 From the rising of the sun to its setting the name of the LORD is to be praised.

As encouraging and hopeful and enthusiastic as this verse is, I have to ask: What about the nighttime? What about those dark times when God seems far away?

Sometimes God seems so far away. So high above us, so distant, that we can't sense God's presence, we don't see God at work in our lives. How could the God of the universe understand us and our problems and our needs and our fears?

As I write this, I am facing a major life decision. I could go one direction and it would change just about everything in my life and send me to a location and into a calling that I don't know very well, though I believe I could learn and thrive there—if I survive. Or I could go the other direction and either find myself at peace, enjoying and improving the life I already know, or else getting stuck in a dead end and consigning my future to mundane stagnation.

And I can't sense God in this decision either way. I'm getting no nudge or warning, no sense of divine direction or guidance. Nothing. Is God testing me? Letting me make my own way, my own choices, my own mistakes? Is God really there?

Whatever I decide, whichever path I choose, will have huge ramifications that will last the rest of my life. So, God, why are you so far away from me right now?

4 The LORD is high above all nations, and his glory above the heavens.

5 Who is like the LORD our God, who is seated on high,

6 who looks far down on the heavens and the earth?

Yes, that's what I'm feeling now. God is "high above" where I am right now. "Seated on high," God "looks far down." God seems a long, long way away from me. Yet this is when I need God most, right here and now.

But then I discover the original Hebrew meaning of that last verb, "looks far down," and it clicks in: God "makes God's self low to see in the heavens and in the earth." God purposefully decides to lower God's self. God doesn't just look from afar; God humbly, purposefully, comes down to where we are, to see us, to know us, to be with us.

7 He raises the poor from the dust, and lifts the needy from the ash heap,

8 to make them sit with princes, with the princes of his people.

9 He gives the barren woman a home, making her the joyous mother of children. Praise the LORD!

God "makes God's self low" to raise us poor creatures from the dry, empty dust of life. God lifts us needy, barren people up to provide the joy, meaning, and fulfillment we crave in the very dwelling place of God's presence.

God is here, right here with you and me, wherever we find ourselves, whatever we're wrestling with. Ready and waiting to raise us to the heights God has planned for us, wherever they may be, to live and walk and work in righteousness and peace, with praises on our lips.

God, sometimes you do seem so far away, so high up, so distant. And yet I know that you are here with me, you see me and know me. You are at work. Let me trust that today and move forward with you into uncharted realms of following you and living as your servant.

Shakened

Psalm 114

THEMES
God's Power
Trust
Provision
Devastation

1 When Israel went out from Egypt, the house of Jacob from a people of strange language,

2 Judah became God's sanctuary, Israel his dominion.

You know the story: The Israelites worked as slaves in Egypt for many years until Moses confronted the Pharaoh and demanded freedom for his people. It took some supernatural doing involving ten plagues afflicting Egypt, including the coming of the Angel of Death (which passed over the Israelites), but ultimately Israel was let go, crossing the Red Sea and entering a period of wandering before they could enter the Promised Land.

The psalmist beautifully captured the story in just a few verses in this song:

3 The sea looked and fled; Jordan turned back.

4 The mountains skipped like rams, the hills like lambs. . . .

7 Tremble, O earth, at the presence of the LORD, at the presence of the God of Jacob,

8 who turns the rock into a pool of water, the flint into a spring of water.

What strikes me in reading this is the beautifully poetic language about the response of the land before the power of God. The sea "saw" the Israelites approaching under the direction of God's mighty power–and ran away. Even the mountains and hills seemed to skip away in fear before the presence of God. The earth trembled and quaked before the Lord.

Can you imagine what it would feel like to be fleeing from Egyptian armies, coming to the brink of a wide sea, and watching the sea and the land open up before you under the hand of God? What must it have looked like and felt like to be in the midst of such a cataclysm?

While the psalm is a beautifully poetic explanation of the power of God, it had to be a terrifying, overwhelming, and confusing experience. And as I read these lines about mountains skipping and seas fleeing, I can't help but think about all the various natural disasters that have devastated hundreds of thousands of people around the world today.

Not long ago as I write this, a cyclone careened through Myanmar decimating the population. An earthquake shook an area of China that left whole villages—including school buildings filled with young children—as piles of rubble. Tornadoes have wreaked havoc in areas all across the United States destroying family homes and whole towns. Tomorrow, we may learn of some new cataclysmic event, reminding us of the fragility of the planet and its inhabitants, and of the often destructive power of the natural world. And we tremble.

Where is God in such times? Where is the powerful Lord who is at work to provide for the people?

Let the words of this psalm remind us that God is wherever there is natural upheaval, wherever the earth trembles.

God is there in all the responses of people around the world to send food, clothing, medical aid, and other support to the devastated regions.

God is there in all the little miracles of survival and courage and sacrifice and care.

God is there in the prayers of the people working on the scene sacrificially to deal with needs of which we may have no comprehension.

God is there, turning the rock into a pool of cool, clean water.

And maybe we are there too.

God, I read the stories of your amazing works in the Bible, and wonder where you are in this hurting, broken, devastated world. Remind me that you are here, and you are at work—through me and through all believers whom you call on to give and pray for and serve those who are in desperate need. Make me aware of ways I can do that—so others can see your power and love in action.

Distracted

Psalm 115

THEMES
Idols
Hindrances
Dedication
Focus

2 Why should the nations say, "Where is their God?"

3 Our God is in the heavens; he does whatever he pleases.

4 Their idols are silver and gold, the work of human hands.

5 They have mouths, but do not speak; eyes, but do not see.

6 They have ears, but do not hear; noses, but do not smell.

7 They have hands, but do not feel; feet, but do not walk; they make no sound in their throats.

8 Those who make them are like them; so are all who trust in them. . . .

In the time the psalmist wrote, the people of God were surrounded by tribes and kingdoms and nations, each of which had their own assortment of gods and idols. Israel was called upon to love and serve the one true God, and forbidden to make any image of that God, as their neighbors—the "nations"—did.

The psalmist compares the God of Israel with the gods of all those nations. Hey, what right do those guys have to challenge us about our God? Sure, they may have all sorts of strange representations of their so-called gods—idols made of precious metals, beautiful and fearsome to look at. But those idols are powerless. They cannot speak, or see, or hear or smell or feel or walk or act or love. There is no wisdom, power, love, or any emotion there. They are simply pieces of sculpture, just sitting there. They may be precious and expensive, but they're ultimately worthless and unreal. We are incapable of relating to them in any personal way, or they to us.

Of course, we hardly ever have to deal with false, powerless, unreal idols in this day and age. Right?

Think about it. Those idols were distractions and diversions from genuine spirituality. Since they were inanimate, one simply could not have a true relationship with these idol gods—and relationship is the core of genuine religion. So they absorbed attention that would much more fruitfully be paid to the true God. They served as hindrances to entering into a meaningful relationship with the One who loves and empowers and calls us to serve.

When you look at it that way, you can't help but see similar idols in our midst today. Perhaps we become so focused on our career—and the status and wealth it brings—that we lose the sense of who we are as God's child. Or it could be that we are so absorbed in our relationship with another person that we become unbalanced in our priorities. It could even be that we become so caught up in some cultural phenomenon—the latest social website or online game, the hottest TV series, the latest frivolous series of books—that we lose life-giving contact with God.

Maybe it's a hobby, a sport, a downtime pleasure, whatever—none of which is bad in itself. They may be a fun and even healthy part of life. But if we fail to keep them in balance, compatible with our life's calling as people who are in deep connection with God, then they become hindrances. Idols. They may be nice and pretty and interesting, but they are incapable of relating to us in any personal way. They have no ultimate meaning.

Let's listen to the psalmist and keep focused on who we are. And who God is. When we do, all these aspects of life will fall into their proper place. And we can join with the psalmist and sing:

11 You who fear the LORD, trust in the LORD! He is their help and their shield.

God, I'll admit I get distracted from all sorts of things I should be doing by things that may not necessarily be bad, but which keep me from being and doing what brings me the most joy and meaning and fulfillment in life—knowing and serving you. Open my eyes today to areas of my life that are keeping me from what's best.

Cherished

THEMES

Death

Love

Celebration

Faithfulness

12 What shall I return to the LORD for all his bounty to me?

13 I will lift up the cup of salvation and call on the name of the LORD,

14 I will pay my vows to the LORD in the presence of all his people.

15 Precious in the sight of the LORD is the death of his faithful ones.

A sweet attendant wearing a flowery blouse, white Keds, and blue scrub pants hustles efficiently around the skeletal body. Then she turns the thermostat on the hospice room's air conditioner all the way to the left, to cold. Very cold. I realize she is turning the room into a cooler until the hearse can come from the funeral home.

My mother is dead.

I had been to West Virginia to see her twice in the previous month or so when she had started to dwindle rapidly; it had been a shock both times to see how she had wasted away in the meantime. This time I had come back to the hospice to join my sister, brothers, and a niece as we waited for the end.

Mom's body is as delicate as an empty seashell. She no longer looks like my beautiful mother, the pretty sister. Her mouth is wide open as she breathes deeply, harshly. Her eyes are closed, they do not move. I have gotten there just in time, it seems.

We gather around her and stroke her face and her hair, matted down already by continual love rubs. An oddly sweet odor permeates the room, the smell of a dying body full of cancer.

It is my niece who urges us to say something to her, to pray for her. My oldest brother and I hardly know where to begin, what to say. He says a few awkward words. I can do no better.

We go in cycles, gathering around, telling her how much we love her and appreciate her, telling her we'll take care of each other and Dad, who lies ill himself in another nursing home. We shed a few tears, and then we sit back down to read whatever we have to distract us for a while. Then we gather around her and do it all again. By the end she is probably wishing we would all just hush.

Wednesday turns into Thursday and we keep waiting. Finally, Friday. Now her eyes move slightly and are open slivers. She seems not only to hear, but to want to respond to us, her mouth almost imperceptibly moves as though she wants to say something. Even her coloring is better.

At one point I am alone with Mom. Again I stroke her face and her hair and kiss her waxy cheek, and tell her how proud I am to be her son, and how thankful I am for her love. I pass along the love of my own family, even her great-grandson and soon to be born great-granddaughter. I tell her how soon she will see her beloved mother and father, the sisters who died before her, her grandson—so many family members and friends and loved ones, waiting.

As I speak to her, I realize she begins to breathe differently. Soon my family members return and I point this out. Once again we gather around her to express our love and our thanks and our good-byes. Her breaths come slower and slower. We call a nurse. After a quick check, she leaves us alone for the final moments.

Finally, one last gulp of breath. And that is it.

Her forehead stays warm a long time. But in an instant, her body looks entirely different. Totally still. Totally empty. Mom is gone. But what a life she left us.

Each of us has lost people who are precious and vital in our lives. Who would you remember and celebrate today? Whose memory fills you with warmth and joy? Whose life of faith and purpose transmitted the same to you? Whose example do you hold up before you as a guide to living fully in the presence of God?

15 *Precious in the sight of the LORD is the death of his faithful ones.*

God, I remember the loved ones in my life, my family, my friends, who have entered into your presence. They were precious to me, they are precious to you. Cherished above all things. Thank you for their faithful witness over the years. May I also be found faithful, and may my life reveal it in many ways.

Determined

Psalm 119

THEMES
Seeking God
Obedience
God's Word
Study
Meditation
Purity

9 *How can young people keep their way pure?*
By guarding it according to your word.

10 *With my whole heart I seek you; do not let*
me stray from your commandments.

11 *I treasure your word in my heart, so that I*
may not sin against you.

12 *Blessed are you, O LORD; teach me your statutes.*

13 *With my lips I declare all the ordinances of your mouth.*

14 *I delight in the way of your decrees as much as in all riches.*

15 *I will meditate on your precepts, and fix my eyes on your ways.*

16 *I will delight in your statutes; I will not forget your word.*

She was angry and frustrated with God. Since college she had been trying to follow the rules and do the right things to fulfill her life dreams—and they weren't outrageous by any stretch of the imagination. But she kept running into speed bumps and roadblocks and even a few brick walls. She had prayed—on her knees!—that God would work out the difficult situation she was currently immersed in—a job that barely paid enough to cover the bare essentials, health insurance that was virtually worthless at a time when she needed some medical attention for her very young children. An opportunity opened up for a full-time job she thought she would do well with. She trusted God. She believed God. But it too became yet another closed door.

Why was life so hard? Why didn't God smooth things out? Why weren't her prayers answered? Why didn't she get what she needed here? She was trying so hard but all she seemed to get were more problems and fewer resources to deal with them. She wanted to enjoy her youth and begin to experience some measure of achievement in life, but this latest setback made her feel she would waste her youth in a sea of despair.

In our youth it's natural when facing difficult circumstances or major disappointments to give up and seek an easy way out, or some way to feel better, or even to give up our responsibilities and run away. But that's not the response of maturity. And maturity can only come by trusting God in the process of walking step by step into the fears and frustrations of everyday life, beginning in our younger years.

The psalmist offers some advice for young people of any age as they contemplate life and its challenges, and while it may come off as simplistic and idealistic and unrealistic, it's still worth meditating on and living into.

These verses come from Psalm 119, the longest chapter in the Bible. It's all about how focusing one's life on the word of God can provide direction and solace and insight and anything else you may need to get through this earthly existence. And this particular section focuses on young people—but we are all young when it comes to how much we need to learn about life.

It's a question we should all ask, one that young woman asked herself time and again: How can we keep our way of living pure and clean and right?

The psalmist suggests that by determining to study, meditate on, and absorb God's word, by following God's example of love and service rather than trying to force life into our own expectations and desires, we can come to live a delighted life.

Anglican priest Jim Cotter summarizes this section of Psalm 119 this way: "The path is tough, and, despite boundary marks, we wander from it. We become self-centered; we ignore others on the path. We are constantly invited to love others as Christ has loved us: that degree of love is not easy for it challenges us to bless, pray for, and help those who are hostile to us."[27]

Maybe that is the way of living a clean, delighted life: by knowing God's way so thoroughly that it can't help but come through every word we say and every action we take—loving and serving wholeheartedly, primarily, and purely. And so no matter what life brings our way, even if we don't see God in it, we know God is actively, intimately with us.

Let's all take a deep breath and examine through the lens of God's word our desires and motives, our expectations of life, our hopes and dreams. Where are we going? How are we getting there? How are we making our way pure?

God, help me to wrestle with those questions today with your wisdom and ways at the front of my mind and heart. Help me to see where my own desires and dreams are pulling me off track. Open my eyes to the needs of others around me so that I can respond unselfishly with your love.

Kept

Psalm 121

THEMES
Protection
Help
Provision
Care

¹ I lift up my eyes to the hills—from where will my help come?

² My help comes from the LORD, who made heaven and earth.

³ He will not let your foot be moved; he who keeps you will not slumber.

⁴ He who keeps Israel will neither slumber nor sleep.

⁵ The LORD is your keeper; the LORD is your shade at your right hand.

⁶ The sun shall not strike you by day, nor the moon by night.

⁷ The LORD will keep you from all evil; he will keep your life.

⁸ The LORD will keep your going out and your coming in from this time on and forevermore.

Did you notice how frequently various forms of the word "keep" occur in this psalm? Go back and count them. The message is clear: God is our keeper.

But I have a little trouble with the word "keeper." When I hear that word I think of a zookeeper, and God certainly must sometimes feel like one of those, having to deal with the human race. I also think of the murderous Cain's complaint to God. When asked where his brother Abel was, Cain countered with, "[A]m I my brother's keeper?" (Gen. 4:9). He obviously didn't think so.

So what does this word "keep" mean?

The Hebrew root word translated "keep" means to guard, to protect, to take care of someone or something. It implies looking out for someone else's best interests, keeping another from harm or injury, watching out for his or her welfare. In order to "keep" someone in this way you must pay attention. You have to intentionally regard the other seriously, personally, continually. You have to care.

God is our keeper. God keeps us in God's constant sight, protecting us always. God keeps us from evil. God keeps us surrounded by care and provision.

The flip side of this concept is that we are God's "kept people." Some people may consider this an imposition, an unwanted inhibition of their freedom and self-determination. To be "kept" by God constrains them. You may know of someone in a relationship who felt "kept" by another, and it is not very often a comfortable place to be.

The same soul friction we may feel if we sense we're being "controlled" by someone else, if we feel a loss of freedom in the way we live, can also apply to our relationship with God, if we let it.

As one "kept" by God we may feel we have to do right, act perfectly, fall in lockstep with others. We may feel forced to fit a certain image, do things a certain way, hold a particular attitude, or even carry an angelic expression on our face at all times.

But that's not what having God as your keeper is about.

God keeps you safe and free to become who you are supposed to be.

God chooses to guard you from whatever eats away at your faith.

God protects you from harm and evil in order to nurture you to become utterly and uniquely you.

God keeps you because God made you and loves you and wants you to be free to live and love to the fullest.

This is the God you can be connected to through faith and trust your whole life long. This is the God who keeps you forever.

God, keep me in the warm palm of your hand. Keep me in the loving gaze of your eyes. Keep me on the path of growth and maturity. Keep me from hurting myself, or putting myself in situations that open me up to harm. Keep me in my going out and my coming in. Keep me forever.

Surrounded

THEMES
Protection
Care
Trust
Strength

1 Those who trust in the LORD are like Mount Zion, which cannot be moved, but abides forever.

2 As the mountains surround Jerusalem, so the LORD surrounds his people, from this time on and forevermore.

I grew up in the Mountain State, West Virginia. In my first job out of college, I worked on a newspaper in a small town in the Cherry River Valley, not far from the state's eastern border with Virginia. It was a gorgeous place, with magnificent steeply wooded hills surrounding the one-traffic-light town along the meandering rocky river. In the autumn the brightly painted leaves, which embraced you in every direction, would literally take your breath away, and in the spring the fresh green of new life was invigorating. It felt like being in the midst of a spectacular landscape painting by a master artist. Safe, secure, immovable. Surrounded by peace and protection.

When I was in Rio de Janeiro, I stood on the roof of my hotel building and looked around in all directions at the green mountains that jutted abruptly into the sky. They surrounded me in every direction; even out to sea they broke through the plane of water to cut a jagged pattern against the horizon. There was Sugarloaf, whose summit I would visit the next day by skycar. And there, behind me, was the Corcovado, the highest point, topped by the awesome sculpture of Christ the Redeemer, whose open-armed embrace reached out to all who gazed up at it.

In both of those places, I was happy, I felt at home. I admired the beauty and strength of the mountains, and felt protected by their embrace.

But I realize that also under the shadow of those mountains in both of those places were people whose lives were marked by poverty. In the hollows of West Virginia, in the favelas of Rio, many suffered hunger and ill health and often lived in fear and emptiness and need. The beauty and grandeur of the circumstances did not necessarily extend protection and security to everyone within their embrace.

How did those hurting folks feel when they looked at the mountains surrounding them? Oppressed? Confined? Overwhelmed? Threatened? Did they feel trapped by their mountainous circumstances?

Or could those people, like the psalmist, sense the divine protection and care that the mountains represented in their massive, immovable embrace?

No matter what our circumstances, we can trust in the Lord. We can choose to accept God's care. We can be as immoveable as those mountains, knowing we are surrounded by God's strength and love. And we can in turn be used by God to help those in our midst who may not be experiencing immovable trust. We can reach out to them and help fulfill their needs in the name of the God who abides forever.

God, I trust in you. This psalm says I therefore cannot be moved; I abide with you forever, as you do with me. Put that trust into action, please. Move me to love and serve in your name.

Rewarded

THEMES
Celebration
Dreams
Joy
Work
Weeping

1 When the LORD restored the fortunes of Zion, we were like those who dream.

2 Then our mouth was filled with laughter, and our tongue with shouts of joy; then it was said among the nations, "The LORD has done great things for them."

3 The LORD has done great things for us, and we rejoiced.

I was far away from home in graduate school in Dallas, Texas, and it was Christmas. With my very young family, I yearned to get back home, see my folks, my brothers and sister, breathe the crisp West Virginia air, watch the local news. I wanted badly to feel at home again, even for just a week or so. But the costs of flying home at that point were prohibitive. And driving from Dallas to Charleston, West Virginia, seemed an overwhelming task with a small baby. It was my dream, but it just didn't seem possible.

But then, just days before the Christmas break, I commiserated with a seminary friend who was pretty much in the same situation. His family was back in North Carolina, and he wanted to take his own wife and baby home. We were both stuck.

Then we realized that, together, maybe we could make it. We could all pile into one car, drive through the night by alternating drivers, and make it to North Carolina splitting costs. There, one of my family members could pick me and my family up and take us on to West Virginia relatively painlessly. It was a fascinating journey through the South—my friend and his wife were African-American, and even in the late 1970s we got some suspicious looks our way. We had one very sick child along the way, and some bad highway food. But we made it home, at least for a brief while. Our dream had come true. And we rejoiced.

The people of God in the psalmist's day also had a dream to return to their homeland. They'd been taken by force from their "promised land" to a foreign country where they were forced to work as slaves. How they yearned to go home. Years passed . . . decades passed . . . but the dream kept burning in their souls.

And finally, unexpectedly they were given a one-way ticket home. They couldn't believe it. Celebration! They were shot through with joy. Even the people of other nations around them could recognize the hand of their God at work.

But then that's when the hard work began. And their prayers changed.

4 Restore our fortunes, O LORD, like the watercourses in the Negeb.

5 May those who sow in tears reap with shouts of joy.

6 Those who go out weeping, bearing the seed for sowing, shall come home with shouts of joy, carrying their sheaves.

The reality of their dream-come-true was much more difficult than they anticipated. Their land had been laid waste, so they had to rebuild. Other people had taken over their villages and homes. They had no protection from outside enemies, no infrastructure. Their fields were thirsty deserts. They had a lot of work to do.

But they accepted the fact that sometimes in life, even when your dreams come true, you have to keep working even while you weep. You have to keep sowing the seeds despite the hardships in order to reap the harvest of a life well lived. You have to water those seeds with your tears of struggle and pain. In my case, the reality was that my trip home was only temporary. We had to return the same way we'd come and get back to work on our degrees.

Even so, God promises that, in the end, you will come home shouting with joy once again with the resulting bounty.

Sometimes dreams come true in a flash, but that's not often, and it's not without its consequences and ramifications. More likely, dreams come true after years of patient, careful, determined struggle. But the joy that results from that life lasts forever.

God, remind me today that the best things in life, the things that bring deep, eternal joy, take time and work and even some tears. But they're worth it. Help me to keep sowing, knowing that you will in your time turn my weeping into shouts of joy.

Doubtful

Psalm 128

THEMES
Promise
Blessing
Happiness
Difficulties
Disasters
Pain

1 Happy is everyone who fears the LORD, who walks in his ways.

2 You shall eat the fruit of the labor of your hands; you shall be happy, and it shall go well with you.

3 Your wife will be like a fruitful vine within your house; your children will be like olive shoots around your table.

4 Thus shall the man be blessed who fears the LORD.

There have been times in my life when I have read this psalm and thought, "Oh yeah?"

Sometimes, perhaps even now, it seems too simplistic. Unrealistic. And in my life experience of trying to walk in the ways of God, I can have very serious doubts.

Then I think, wouldn't it be great if it were so? I've known people who come close to this portrait of happy faithful living, but then are devastated by an unexpected tragedy. Or financial reversals wipe them out. Or a child descends into the world's darkness never to emerge again.

We want so badly to be a living example of the image of this psalm, but it seems so far away, almost unreachable. How do we deal with this? How do we read this lovely psalm about simple faith and the promised benefits thereof and compare it with our own lives and the suffering and pain and frustration we are forced to deal with at times? Is this a fairy tale? Is it all a sham?

New Yorker critic James Wood, in a review of the book *God's Problem* by Bart Ehrman, explored the question of why God permits suffering, especially in the lives of the righteous. He cited a single recent day that brought news of earthquakes, cyclones, bomb attacks in Iraq, Northern Spain, and Pakistan, and on and on and on. How can this happen if there is a God of love? "For the lucky few," Wood writes, "there is reason to hope that life will be a business of evenly rationed suffering. . . . Plenty of suffering for a life, certainly, but most of us subsist on the plausible expectation that fortune [or God?] will draw a circle around the personal portion, and that the truly unbearable—murder, rape, dead children, torture, war—will remain outside the cordon."[28]

But these lucky are indeed very few, it seems. Wood reviews the major teachings of Judaism and Christianity, which over the millennia have attempted to explain this problem of suffering, and then concludes: "The problem for Jews is that the Messiah never came, and everything stayed the same (or got worse), while the problem for Christians is that the Messiah did come, and everything stayed the same (or got worse)."[29]

The disturbing thing to me is that Wood makes some good points. But the gut-level truth is that I'm not ready to toss my faith over the side over this. I may have doubts and lots of questions, but I know there is some substance and reality to my faith.

Here's the reality: We all have doubts, and we need to dive into them and feel them and examine them and work through them. Hiding from them or denying them only causes them to fester in our soul. Let's be honest. Let's talk about them. Let's share our own experiences, and see what God says to us in the process. Let's let God do God's work in our lives through it all.

Then we can read these verses and let them seep into our minds and hearts. We can see them as an ideal to aim for, realistically. We can learn to be happy, truly happy, in whatever circumstances we find ourselves.

There is great blessing in living like that in the fear of the Lord.

God, I yearn for the blessed life pictured in this psalm. But the reality of my life, and of the hurting, fractured world around me, gives me pause. I don't want to doubt your loving promise, but I do want to be honest and realistic. And I do want my faith to be strong and authentic. Something tells me that a faith like that is only forged in the crucible of real life.

Pardoned

THEMES

Forgiveness

Sin

Waiting

Hope

Prayer

Mercy

¹ Out of the depths I cry to you, O LORD.

² Lord, hear my voice! Let your ears be attentive to the voice of my supplications!

They sit in padded folding chairs in an irregular circle. They are of various ages and backgrounds and races, facing one another, and facing their fears. They take turns sharing personally about family members or friends who are in intensive outpatient rehab for drugs or alcohol. Each story touches on intense fear, devastation, and the repercussions of the multitude of poor choices their loved ones have made, the addictions that now ravage them.

Someone says, "I don't know if she's hit rock bottom yet. You would think, having lost her children, her husband, her job, her home—that would be rock bottom, but it doesn't seem to be. What is rock bottom? For me rock bottom would have been a long time ago."

The group leader says, "Rock bottom is whatever rock bottom is for each person. They don't know it's rock bottom until they get there."

Rock bottom. The depths. The gutter. Some of us have been there. Others of us have beloved family members or friends who have been there—or are there now. It is the chaos of a life lived apart from trust in God.

There is no need to wait for rock bottom to cry out to God. To acknowledge how you've broken the relationship with God and set out on your own way. To admit that you have failed—yourself, your loved ones, your God. But even if you are in the lowest, most chaotic depths of human experience, God can hear your cry:

³ If you, O Lord, should mark iniquities, Lord, who could stand?

⁴ But there is forgiveness with you, so that you may be revered.

⁵ I wait for the LORD, my soul waits, and in his word I hope.

The psalmist acknowledges that he or she has sinned, has messed up totally. And if God let that situation stand, there would be no hope. Even rock bottom would shatter and give way to a bottomless pit.

But "there is forgiveness with you." Even in the depths, God is with you. You are with God, who hears and waits to pardon those who honestly ask for it.

As J. K. Rowling, creator of Harry Potter, said in a 2008 Harvard commencement speech, that after she had "failed on an epic scale" in life, "I was set free, because my greatest fear had already been realized, and I was still alive, and I still had a daughter whom I adored, and I had an old typewriter and a big idea. And so rock bottom became the solid foundation on which I rebuilt my life."[30]

It may take some time. You may have to wait. But you can wait in hope.

God, it's easy to be so consumed and distracted by the depths surrounding me that I don't see your hand of forgiveness stretching out to me. Let me get honest with myself, and with you. I know I need forgiveness, as a first step toward moving back up. I wait for that pardon expectantly.

Quieted

THEMES
Peace
Calm
Quiet
Stress
Humility
Panic

I was riding the MARTA train home from the airport after a trip, watching as a young Latina with two young sons, one maybe three, the other less than a year old, sat across from me. The younger, in a stroller, was not happy at all. Anxious, tired, frustrated, who knows what emotions coursed through his mind. He began crying and arching his back in an attempt to free himself from his bonds. She glanced at me and smiled with embarrassment. I smiled back in sympathy because I had seen that arched-back anger and frustration in my own children and grandchildren many, many times over the years.

Then she pulled her young son out of his stroller. He still fought and arched and struggled, until she pulled out a bottle of milk and brought it to his lips. Immediately he dissolved into his mother's cradling arms and lay there contentedly. The emotions drained away from him blissfully, even in the midst of the racket of the train and the bustling passengers around him.

I thought of that mother and child when I read Psalm 131.

1 O LORD, my heart is not lifted up, my eyes are not raised too high;
I do not occupy myself with things too great and too marvelous for me.

2 But I have calmed and quieted my soul, like a weaned child with its
mother; my soul is like the weaned child that is with me.

Just hours before I rode the MARTA train home, I was in a taxi on the way to the Minneapolis/St. Paul airport after participating in a weeklong preaching conference. A big sign flashed on the side of the road just ahead of the exit for the airport: "Terror Level: Code Orange" it read. That's all. Everyone who saw that sign knew what it meant, and I will admit to a flash of fear in my heart when I saw it. How I would have liked to have folded up into the fetal position and experienced the calm and quiet of a mother's love at that moment.

Just a couple of days before at the conference, I had heard scholar Walter Brueggemann refer to this psalm, saying that its message to us is an encouragement to choose not to live as under an Orange Alert, but to live in the knowledge that God sees us and knows us in our distress, and offers motherly comfort to us—the calm and quiet of a child with its mother.[31]

That requires intentionality and acceptance on our part. Rather than arching our back in fear or frustration or exhaustion or hunger, let's relax in the comforting arms of God. Let us take in the sustaining peace only God can give us.

God, I realize that not arching my back against my distressing circumstances requires humility on my part. Surrendering. Allowing you to hold me. Letting myself go in your arms. Taking in your healing nourishment. Which then enables me to grow up just a little more, and learn to do what I can to make this world a more peaceful and loving place.

United

THEMES

Community

Siblinghood

Blessing

Peace

Unity

Family

¹ How very good and pleasant it is when kindred live together in unity!

² It is like the precious oil on the head, running down upon the beard, on the beard of Aaron, running down over the collar of his robes.

³ It is like the dew of Hermon, which falls on the mountains of Zion. For there the LORD ordained his blessing, life forevermore.

Years ago when I was struggling through numerous personal, professional, and spiritual battles, and began drifting away from my adopted conservative evangelical faith, which I had tried so hard to make work, I accidentally found my way to a new church home. I can remember the first Sunday I attended this church, which was so different from anything I had ever experienced before. Even the order of worship was new to me, let alone the lovely and moving music, the welcoming spirit, and the intellectually rigorous sermon that made more sense than just about anything I had heard in the previous decade and a half.

Suddenly, surprisingly, I was home.

In this vibrant Episcopal parish I found new meaning and direction in life, and ultimately deep challenges to the way I had been living my life. And one of the aspects of this community that was so powerful to me was the fact that the members represented a broad range of theological views, from staunchly conservative to radically progressive. Which made for some lively Sunday school classes and small groups. And yet they were able, willing, and even eager to gather together around the altar and celebrate the Eucharist together as brothers and sisters in Christ. They were family, and they loved one another despite whatever differences they might have. As the rector, Gray Temple, explained to me, Episcopalians are a sacramental, rather than a creedal, people. They bonded around the Eucharist rather than a set of doctrines.

This made sense to me. This seemed to be the way it was supposed to be. You didn't have to agree with everyone else to be accepted and even loved. It was indeed "good and pleasant."

But over the years the rector began to press the issue of gay marriage with his flock. This was a full decade or more before the Episcopal Church as a whole fully began to engage the issue, resulting in a few splits and departures at all levels. Our rector was making waves early, and a lot of people were deeply offended by his progressive, welcoming views.

And yet, after several months of angry and hurtful disagreement, things seemed to be settling down. The church family had made it through other major disagreements before and managed largely to stay together. Maybe, somehow, they could weather this storm as well. But then, an all-church meeting led by the then-bishop seemed to enflame those who disagreed with the concept of welcoming gays and lesbians and blessing their unions, and the flight was on. A good number of the congregational family left to attend other churches or even to create a new one.

It was heartbreaking, and it took me a couple of years to work my way through that cataclysmic event personally, as some folks I was deeply close to then chose to leave. I even left for a while, but felt myself drawn back home—not only to my church home, but back home to myself.

For a brief time, this psalm seemed to picture real life in this congregation. But perhaps it's only human. We will always have differences and disagreements that separate us. In our families, our churches, our communities, our nation, our world.

But having experienced it, I want to work toward that image of abundant love and goodness flowing down. I guess it does start with me, doesn't it? And you.

God, I want to make a difference in fostering loving, accepting unity wherever I am, in my family, my neighborhood, my church, my nation. Please give me the tender strength I need to reach out and accept others whoever they may be. And love them in your name.

Remembered

THEMES

Love
Faithfulness
Acceptance
Rescue
Provision
Thanksgiving
Eternity

¹ O give thanks to the LORD, for he is good, for his steadfast love endures forever.

² O give thanks to the God of gods, for his steadfast love endures forever.

³ O give thanks to the Lord of lords, for his steadfast love endures forever;

⁴ who alone does great wonders, for his steadfast love endures forever; . . .

One night my condo neighbor was having yet another party. His stereo was on and all I could hear as I lay in my bed trying to sleep was the bassie beat of the music. All I could hear. Pounding in my brain. Not quite loud enough to complain (and, I'll admit, I'd been over there twice in the past around midnight to complain), but loud enough to just drive me up the wall, which is not a comfortable place to sleep after a long, hard workweek.

I pulled out a pair of earplugs that I use when the sounds of the city or the neighbors intrude more than I can stand. Most of the noise is filtered out, at least enough so that my brain can relax and I can fall asleep. But when I first started using them, the sound I heard instead was a little strange. It was relentless. It was overwhelming even.

It was the sound of my own pulse in my ears. At first, it was almost worse than the noise I was trying to block out. My heartbeat was deep, constant, loud, unrelenting.

But then I fell into the cadence. Maybe I let myself remember being in the womb and hearing my mother's heartbeat. The sound became a calming sensation. Reassuring. Comforting. Like the refrain in this psalm.

²³ It is he who remembered us in our low estate, for his steadfast love endures forever;

²⁴ and rescued us from our foes, for his steadfast love endures forever;

²⁵ who gives food to all flesh, for his steadfast love endures forever.

²⁶ O give thanks to the God of heaven, for his steadfast love endures forever.

Read this whole psalm and you'll hear the heartbeat. The pulse of God's love. Ever beating, never stopping, always pulsing:

God's steadfast love endures forever.

God's steadfast love endures forever.

God's steadfast love endures forever.

Can you hear it? Can you know it and feel it?

Let this refrain remind you always, continually, repeatedly, that God loves you. Despite our weaknesses and failures, despite our circumstances and our struggles, despite our doubts and our fears, God's faithfulness is unwavering, God's love is unchanging.

God remembers you. You are always on God's mind, whether God is on yours. God has remembered you in the past when you were low, as well as in times of triumph, because God steadfastly loves you.

God rescues you from your enemies, internally and externally. God liberates you from your difficulties and fears, because God steadfastly loves you.

God provides your every need in life, from physical nourishment to spiritual nurture, food for life we can enjoy and share together, because God steadfastly loves you.

And what is our response? We can take it all for granted. We can forget that it's true, or doubt it. We can acknowledge it with a casual nod. Or we can make our life a song of gratitude for the God of heaven, who loves us, remembers us, rescues us and provides for us.

When you learn to hear the heartbeat of God's love for you throughout your day, you can deal with anything. Even noisy neighbors.

God, thank you for the reminder that you love me, now and always. Help me to hear the beat of that loving refrain no matter how loud the world gets around me. I give thanks to you, God of heaven, for your steadfast love that endures forever.

Wonderfully Made

THEMES
Identity
Creation
Personality
Sexuality
Acceptance

¹ O LORD, you have searched me and known me.

² You know when I sit down and when I rise up; you discern my thoughts from far away.

³ You search out my path and my lying down, and are acquainted with all my ways.

⁴ Even before a word is on my tongue, O LORD, you know it completely. . . .

Is there anyone who doesn't wonder what on earth God was thinking when we were created? Why did God make us look like this, or act like that, or . . . *be* that?

Life can be one long struggle for self-acceptance. In some ways, that struggle never ends. But if we can get to the point of acceptance, of integrity, of being who we were created to be—whatever that may be—it's amazing what God can do. Our self-destructive war over our identity ends, and we can begin to live into a new truth, the truth of who we are, and serve God out of that truth in exciting and fulfilling ways.

The starting point is understanding what the psalmist is saying here. God has searched us and known us. We're not hiding anything from God. Every aspect of our being—our sitting and standing, our lying down, even our thoughts—it's all well and fully known by God. God knows all our ways. God even knows what we're going to say before our tongue can form the words. And how does God know all that about us?

¹³ For it was you who formed my inward parts; you knit me together in my mother's womb.

¹⁴ I praise you, for I am fearfully and wonderfully made.

That doesn't mean we should blame God for the things about ourselves we don't care for or can't stand. That means we should learn to accept every part of us as fashioned lovingly and knowingly by God, from our physical features, our personality quirks, our inherent skills and abilities (or lack thereof), our sexual orientation—every aspect that makes us who we uniquely are.

That knowledge—which the psalmist says is "too wonderful to me . . . so high I cannot attain it" (v. 6)—can truly set us free. Here's one example:

Brett Webb-Mitchell is a minister and university professor who, after a lifelong internal struggle, finally came to grips with his true identity as a gay man. So what was it that finally made everything click? "It was Psalm 139 that finally convinced me to be who I am," he said in an interview. "You are constructed by God; you are wonderfully made. . . . I am who God made me."[32]

What is it that this psalm might convince you about concerning yourself? How might it encourage you to be who you are, whatever that means? It may not be your sexual orientation you are having trouble accepting—there are plenty of other aspects of your identity and personality that can bring you concern or even grief. And this isn't an excuse for bad habits, laziness, or getting set in your ways.

This is about being you, wonderfully you, and loving and serving God out of that distinctive, authentic identity wherever God takes you.

God, I do thank you for making me, me. Sometimes I don't feel so wonderfully made. And sometimes I really don't want you searching and knowing me. But if I'm honest with myself, and with you, then I can find comfort in that fact. You do know me. And you love me completely anyway. Help me to begin to see myself as you see me, so that I can in turn help others experience more fully who they are as children of God and followers of our loving Lord.

Championed

THEMES
Neediness
Justice
Poverty
Trust
Righteousness

12 I know that the LORD maintains the cause of the needy, and executes justice for the poor.

13 Surely the righteous shall give thanks to your name; the upright shall live in your presence.

The psalmist's message is clear: God is the champion of the needy. And if we want to live in the presence of God, we must have justice for the poor and needy on our hearts—and that means on our agendas too.

So why do we have so much trouble finding the time and energy to engage in serving the poor and needy? Perhaps it's because we ignore the need. We look the other way. We avoid confronting the problem—or allowing it to confront us.

It starts with making eye contact.

Mike Kinman, a priest who has always seemed to be a champion of God's justice in action, helps us take that first step.

"Not making eye contact," Kinman says in a sermon, "is the mantra of urban living . . . when we make eye contact with someone, we make a connection. We establish relationship. We invite them into our lives. When we do that, we become vulnerable . . . and vulnerability compromises safety."

"Christ's call to us to make eye contact," he continues, "is to venture into the neighborhoods of poverty and literally to look the 'we' who live there in the eyes, and listen to them and learn from them, . . . not to drive by or drive around but to gaze on people on society's margins with compassion, to bind their wounds and love them extravagantly."[33]

Mike knows, just as this psalmist knew, that God is the champion of the poor and the needy. And God calls us to take part in this work in righteousness.

So what will you do about it? How will you join the Lord's cause?

Will you seek ways not only to support efforts to feed and clothe the poor financially, but through your personal involvement?

Will you become more involved in your church's or community's outreach efforts to serve—and to be with—the homeless and hungry in your neighborhood or city?

Will you take care to learn all you can about where the clothes you purchase are made—and how they're made and by whom?

Will you make the effort to determine where your financial investments are put to work, and how they affect the livelihood of those who struggle to survive?

Will you become well versed on the Millennium Development Goals and learn what needs to be done to fulfill them and how you can be part of that?

Will you be a champion too?

God, you make clear that the poor and the needy are always on your heart. The psalmist says you maintain their cause, you execute justice on their behalf. But I realize that the way you do that involves me and my brothers and sisters. Make me more aware of the need and how I can be used to help meet it in your love and strength.

Guarded

THEMES

Words

Actions

Evil

Prayer

Righteousness

¹ I call upon you, O LORD; come quickly to me; give ear to my voice when I call to you.

² Let my prayer be counted as incense before you, and the lifting up of my hands as an evening sacrifice.

³ Set a guard over my mouth, O LORD; keep watch over the door of my lips.

- The pressure is rising and you can feel your temperature rising with it. Frustrations build, there's too much going on, and you are feeling your control slip away. You're this close to lashing out with hurtful, angry words just to relieve some of the pressure, but causing more problems as a result . . .

- Someone at work has told you something in confidence, and you know that if only your superior knew this, it could help you get that promotion you've been hoping for. It's bound to come out anyway, right? So why not help the process along?

- Someone is sharing something that's obviously important to her, something you think is silly, and you let her know, in a little too snide and snarky way, just what you think of it.

- You get some disappointing news from someone who can't do what he said he would—yes, he has a great excuse, but it's still disappointing, and you let your disappointment overwhelm you and snap at him in your hurt, only making the hurt worse. . . .

Let's see, check, check, check, check. Yes, I've been faced by all of those situations the past week or so. How about you?

⁴ Do not turn my heart to any evil, to busy myself with wicked deeds in company with those who work iniquity; do not let me eat of their delicacies.

The words we speak can be healing, or destructive. They can build up, or tear down. They can be wise, or foolish.

We can utter prayers that rise as fragrant incense to God. We can mutter curses and bitter words that hurt. And once those hurtful words are spoken, it's impossible to erase them or take them back.

The psalmist knew this and asked God to help. *"Set a guard over my mouth, O LORD; keep watch over the door of my lips."*

That doesn't remove the responsibility from our shoulders, but it can give us the wisdom and strength to measure our words before we speak them.

And turn it around. When someone is speaking to you and you sense that, under pressure, they're falling into some unthinking talk that could potentially hurt you, ask God for understanding. Detach yourself and try to understand why they're saying what they're saying. There may be a good bit of truth to what they say, but maybe they're not saying it well for whatever reason.

In such cases, instead of reacting in anger or hurt, try responding in love. That requires prayer too.

A simple phone conversation I was having with a friend one time began to escalate and touch on some sensitive subjects. It escalated to the point that we began shouting charges and countercharges at each other. Neither of us would change our position on the issue, and if that was so, how could we continue to be friends?

I was stunned that what I assumed was simply an everyday conversation had taken this sharp turn downhill. The result was that we had, somehow, suddenly decided to end the friendship over the issue. Just like that.

Of course the relationship was strong enough that we soon resolved our differences. We met a few days later to talk through it, having both realized the foolishness of our quick verbal assaults on each other. I began to understand why the issue was so important to my friend because of his life experiences, and he began to see my side of things. In distinct contrast to our phone conversation, these words were as fragrant incense, a prayer of praise to God.

If only I had tried to listen more openly, try to understand my friend's reasons, before reacting in anger and hurt. We both learned a lot through this experience, especially how to be more clear in what we were saying and why, and when, and how. To be honest and mutually supportive, to try to understand and accept one another, rather than react argumentatively or hurtfully.

Prepare yourself. Ask God to guard your mouth and your lips.

God, I think of the times I have opened my big mouth before thinking, and how much pain and work it took to overcome the hurt or humiliation. So I pray this prayer of the psalmist's. Help me to wisely, humbly, and lovingly consider my words before I speak.

Happy

THEMES
Happiness
Fulfillment
Mindfulness
Joy
Being Present

1 Praise the LORD! Praise the LORD, O my soul!

2 I will praise the LORD as long as I live; I will sing praises to my God all my life long. . . .

5 Happy are those whose help is the God of Jacob, whose hope is in the LORD their God,

What makes you truly happy? What's on your list?

- Finishing a project on time, and feeling good about it.
- Having a delectable dinner with cherished friends.
- Watching a beautiful sunrise in an unexpected place.
- Seeing a child play in a park playground with abandon.
- Having someone special look into your eyes and say, "I love you."
- Getting the bills paid without overdrawing your bank account.
- Receiving a note of appreciation from someone you admire.
- Watching your garden flourish and enjoying its bounty.
- Listening to a choir sing a majestic anthem.
- Finding yourself in a quiet, peaceful, meditative space.

According to this psalm, happiness belongs to those who choose to follow God, who hope in the Lord. When that relationship is strong, happiness can flow through all sorts of activities and accomplishments in our lives.

And yet, with all the responsibilities, pressures, and fears we face so continually, happiness can be an elusive target. When it does come, we often miss the opportunity to experience it because we aren't paying attention.

In an interview, French psychiatrist Christophe André, who has written often on the subject, provides some helpful guidance for experiencing happiness. He points out that we go through many wonderful times in life but don't experience them as "happy" until later, after they're long gone, when we stop and realize what a good time we had. But we missed being in that moment of happiness. "You need to realize that there are many opportunities to be happy. You have to realize: *This is enjoyable, this is a nice moment, I'm having fun, this is a little bubble of happiness.*"

So often we are unable to experience our happy situation on Sunday evening because we're already thinking about what waits for us at work on Monday morning. And at work we don't experience the happiness of a job well done because we're missing our loved ones at home. We don't live in the present moment. Instead, we need to be where we are, enjoy where we are for this moment, and give ourselves fully to the here and now.

"This can be learned," André says. "The English call it 'mindfulness.' Concentrating helps; meditation is very good. It takes hard work every day, but it works. Happiness can be learned. It's within reach."[34]

We can learn to be happy, to know the happiness we let pass by us without realizing it. It takes being alive, aware, and present in the moment, being mindful of what's happening around us and within us right now.

But true happiness arises from a solid foundation in life. Happiness comes out of relationship with the creative God who keeps faith with us forever, the God to whom we turn naturally and immediately for help and hope. Unless we are grounded in the truth of who we are as a child of God, then true happiness, joy, and fulfillment will elude us.

When we have that relationship, that connection with God, locked in, then those moments of happiness that come into our lives can become more apparent, more real, more often. Because we see our world through eyes of faith.

God, thank you for the little bubbles of happiness you bring into my life. Let me be more aware of them. Let me fully experience them. And let me share them with others in your name.

Brokenhearted

Psalm 147

THEMES
Dreams
Disappointment
Discouragement
Hope
Healing

1 Praise the LORD! How good it is to sing praises to our God; for he is gracious, and a song of praise is fitting.

2 The LORD builds up Jerusalem; he gathers the outcasts of Israel.

3 He heals the brokenhearted, and binds up their wounds.

About ten years ago, an unbelievable dream of mine almost came true. Even now I can hardly believe it came so close to happening.

In *Out of the Quiet*, I wrote about the impact Stan Lee had on my life. Stan, you may have heard, is the co-creator of such comic-book superstars as Spider-Man, Hulk, Fantastic Four, X-Men, Daredevil, and a plethora of others. When I was about nine years old, my big brother Greg gave me a couple of issues featuring Spidey and another favorite of mine, The Mighty Thor. I was entranced. I became enamored of Lee's senses-shattering tales of derring-do and do-gooding. I honestly believe that Lee's philosophy of helping others (as in Spider-Man's motto, "With great power comes great responsibility") and living by the golden rule, which infused his tales, made a mighty impact on my life and faith.

As a kid I used to hole up in my bedroom and write and draw my own comic books. I had big dreams of following in Stan Lee's footsteps. Someday, I thought . . .

Well, dreams die hard. So ten years ago or so, I heard a rumor from a friend that Stan Lee was thinking about writing, of all things, "Christian comic books." What a perfect opportunity for me! I wrote to Stan's halcyon headquarters and offered my services as a writer, since I was both an utter comic book geek, a lifelong Stan fan (even a Permanent Marvelite Maximus!), had a theology degree, and had even had some serious books published.

To my utter amazement, I got a call from Stan's right-hand man, the VP of creative development, who gave me an idea of what Stan had in mind. He wanted to create some super-heroes with a Christian orientation—and by that he meant positive, heroic, self-sacrificial, living a life of positive morality. He felt kids needed good moral examples.

Stan's associate kept in touch over time, and before long we were talking about developing a whole line of comic books featuring such heroes, which might spin off into video games, motion pictures—and I would be writing them under Stan's direction. I was so jazzed. I couldn't believe it!

A few weeks later they sent me a two-page summary of a super-character Stan had created, with a description, background, supporting characters, and possible plot lines and story ideas. I was told that in the next few days we'd set up a conference call with Stan himself to talk through all this and then I could get started writing the first story.

Can you imagine how my inner geek was feeling?

But then I heard nothing. E-mails went unanswered. And before long I learned that Stan's dot-com company was out of business—shut down in the technology bust of the late 1990s.

There came crashing down my lifelong dreams of comic-book stardom. I was heartbroken.

Stan was back at work soon after in other venues, but the line of "Christian comic books" never figured into his new plans for movies and TV shows. Ah well. He continues to be an encouragement to me and never fails to respond to any e-mail I send him within the hour. He's that kind of guy. I even got to meet him in person at his office in LA a few years ago.

I've moved on as well, now doing something I enjoy more than anything else I've done in my life. So it all worked out. God has healed my broken heart. And I have a good story to tell to boot.

How about your broken heart? Your shattered dream? I came across a timely quote about such things: "There are broken hearts and wounded souls in this world. The flowing tear, the pensive look, the deep-drawn sigh are everywhere symptoms of sorrowing souls. The whole human creation is groaning: there are hearts broken by oppression, disappointment, calumny, bereavement, and moral conviction. . . . God works here to remove all this misery—to heal and restore."[35]

I read that and immediately identified with it. And then I found out it's from a sermon preached in the 1850s by a Congregational preacher in North Wales.

Some things never change. Like broken hearts. And God's healing touch, which works constantly to bind up wounds and restore those hearts to wholeness.

Praise the Lord.

God, you know the dreams I've been harboring for so long, the dreams that have been shattered by reality, or never seem to come close to reality, for one reason or another. I'm giving them to you. Heal my broken heart, and build within me new dreams that, in the strength and guidance of the Spirit, can come true.

Enthused

We've been on a long journey together through these psalms, and as we come to the end I hope your connection with God has become deeper and stronger, more real, more hopeful, more challenging. What have we discovered along the way?

1 Praise the LORD! Praise God in his sanctuary; praise him in his mighty firmament!

Together we've learned more about this God who can seem so high above us and far away. We've discovered that even though God is mighty and lofty, God is also right here with us, deeply mindful of us, and steadfastly loving us. This is the God we've come to know and connect with better through these songs of faith. Yet we also realize we haven't come to the end of anything—we're just beginning. We have far to go in this journey of knowing and serving God. But it's a path we yearn to keep traveling. So let's praise the Lord.

2 Praise him for his mighty deeds; praise him according to his surpassing greatness!

Together we've learned more about how God has acted in the past, in the nation Israel, through lives of countless faithful people from ages past as well as in our own times. And we've realized more clearly how God has acted in our own lives to heal us, free us, challenge us, and use us for God's glory. So let's praise the Lord.

3 Praise him with trumpet sound; praise him with lute and harp!

Together we've learned that there are innumerable ways to know, serve, and love God, no matter who we are or what we're up to in life. We've learned that we can express our faith more joyfully and boldly because we've come to acknowledge our unshakable connection with God. And we know that we can join in this song throughout our whole day, at work and at home, in crisis and calm, in conflict and joy, in pain and sadness, in failure and victory. So let's praise the Lord.

4 Praise him with tambourine and dance; praise him with strings and pipe!

Together we've learned that the pain of human existence is real for each one of us. Our struggles may be different but are nevertheless real and demanding, and yet we've come to know that God can work in those struggles to make us more whole, more holy. Whatever it is in life that we're wrestling with or trying to work out, we know that we can deal with it, rise above it, learn from it, and leave it with God. We can even dance. So let's praise the Lord.

5 Praise him with clanging cymbals; praise him with loud clashing cymbals!

Together we've learned that we are all in this together, that we need to be connected with one another in the body of faith, encouraging one another, learning from one another, leaning on one another. We listen, we ask, we pray, we embrace, we serve, we cheer one another on. This is the will of the God who calls us to be one, and who works within us to make life more interesting and fulfilling. So let's praise the Lord.

6 Let everything that breathes praise the Lord! Praise the Lord!

Together we've learned that we need to look beyond our own lives, beyond our closest loved ones, even our congregation, to see the world beyond. We've come to realize we are all part of the life of this world, and that we can make a difference through our witness, our service, our giving. Everything that breathes is precious to God, and we welcome all into our circle, to love and serve them in the power of God. So let's praise the Lord.

What else have you learned in this journey through the psalms? Don't let it stop here. Let your spiritual growth continue day by day in connection with God and one another.

With a connection to God that's unbreakable, you can join in the mighty chorus, uniting with those you're connected to in your church, your community, the whole world, and throughout eternity. You can join in the ageless, endless song of praise with energy, fervor, and enthusiasm, with heartfelt worship and absolute surrender, and be raised to higher levels of spiritual awareness and response.

Make every breath you take, part of the ongoing song that you can sing today and every day. Sing it as long as you have breath to sing it. Now and forevermore.

Let's praise the Lord.

God, I praise you for the connection I have with you, with all who love you, and with all who need you. May you and I keep it strong and alive, day by day, forever.

Endnotes

1. James Wood, "Desert Storm," *New Yorker*, vol. LXXXIII, no. 29 (Oct. 1, 2007): 94.

2. Ibid. 94.

3. Debbie Blue, "Living the Word," *Christian Century*, vol. 125, no. 6 (Mar. 25, 2008): 20.

4. Fred R. Anderson, in a *Day1* Podcast Extra, Feb. 11, 2008, and in another *Day1* recording session on Feb. 21, 2008.

5. "*Annie Hall* (1977): Memorable Quotes," retrieved from http://www.imdb.com/title/tt0075686/quotes.

6. Motoko Rich, "Gang Memoir, Turning Page, Is Pure Fiction," *New York Times* (Mar. 4, 2008), retrieved from http://www.nytimes.com/2008/03/04/books/04fake.html.

7. Daniel Mendelsohn, "Stolen Suffering," *New York Times* (Mar. 9, 2008), retrieved from http://www.nytimes.com/2008/03/09/opinion/09 mendelsohn.html.

8. Dang Thuy Tram, *Last Night I Dreamed of Peace*, trans. Andrew X. Pham (New York: Harmony Books, 2007), 225.

9. Some details from Bruce Cadwallader, "Widow, 94, Clearly Recalls When Husband Was Killed" (Apr. 2, 2008), and "Killer, Braggart Gets 7 to 25 Years" (Apr. 5, 2008), *Columbus Dispatch*, retrieved from http://www.dispatch .com/live/content/local_news/stories/2008/04/02/jenkins.ART_ART_04-02-08_B1_7O9QDKF.html?type=rss&cat=21&sid=101 and http://www.dispatch .com/live/content/local_news/stories/2008/04/05/sjenkins.ART_ART_04-05-08_B1_749RB7G.html?sid=101.

10. Bill Clinton, "Radio Address by the President to the Nation," Marketwire, Dec. 1999, retrieved from http://findarticles.com/p/articles/mi_pwwi/is_199912/ai_mark07991026.

11. Carol Forsloff, "Keep Dancing and Romancing: The Secret to Long Love and Long Life," Associated Content, Nov. 21, 2008, retrieved from http://www.associatedcontent.com/article/1197123/keep_dancing_and_ romancing_the_secret.html?page=1&cat=12.

12. "Polish Man Wakes Up from 19-Year Coma," BBC News (June 2, 2007), retrieved from http://news.bbc.co.uk/2/hi/europe/6715313.stm.

13. Mark Spivak, "Key West: True Indie Spirit." *National Geographic Traveler*, Jan./Feb. 2009, 36.

14. Gene Robinson, *In the Eye of the Storm* (New York: Seabury Books, 2008), 2.

15. "Fannie Mae Forgives Loan for Woman Who Shot Herself," CNN.com, Oct. 3, 2008, retrieved from http://www.cnn.com/2008/US/10/03/eviction.suicide.attempt/index.html.

16. John Swansburg, "HSBC's Bizarre Lumberjack Ad," Slate.com, Oct. 27, 2008. Retrieved from http://www.slate.com/id/2203103/.

17. Charles Swindoll, *Strengthening Your Grip* (Nashville: Thomas Nelson Publishers, 1998).

18. *God's Word* translation (God's Word to the Nations Bible Society, published under license by Baker Book House).

19. "Quicksand Rescue as Boys Sink Up to Necks," *Telegraph (UK)*, Aug. 28, 2007. Retrieved from http://www.telegraph.co.uk/news/uknews/1561516/Quicksand-rescue-as-boys-sink-up-to-necks.html.

20. Daniel Simkins, "God's Will," episode 7 of *The Book of Daniel*.

21. Edward L. Beck, *Soul Provider: Spiritual Steps to Limitless Love* (New York: Doubleday, 2007), 115–20.

22. Stephen Holden, "Fresh Produce for Ratatouille, Please, but No Attitude." *New York Times*, June 8, 2008, retrieved from http://movies.nytimes.com/2008/06/06/movies/06groc.html.

23. Walter Brueggemann, "A Life and a Time Other Than Our Own," lecture delivered at the Festival of Homiletics, May 21, 2008, Minneapolis, MN.

24. Jimmy Moor, "A Place of Welcome," sermon preached on the *Day1* radio program, June 17, 2007, retrieved from http://day1.org/1084-a_place_of_welcome.

25. David Hochman, "The Age of Anxiety." *Details* (Jan./Feb. 2008): 135.

26. Ibid., 135.

27. Jim Cotter, *Psalms for a Pilgrim People* (Harrisburg, PA: Morehouse Publishing), 256.

28. James Wood, "Holiday in Hellmouth." *New Yorker*, vol. LXXXIV, no. 17 (June 9/16, 2008): 116.

29. Ibid., 122.

30. Sam Dillon, "Messages of Exhortation, Counsel and Congratulation," *New York Times* (June 16, 2008): 16.

31. Walter Brueggemann, "A Life and a Time."

32. Leslie Boyd, "Gay Pastor Shares His Parenting Experiences," *Asheville (NC) Citizen-Times* (Jan. 26, 2008), retrieved from http://www.citizen-times.com/apps/pbcs.dll/article?AID=200880124131.

33. Mike Kinman, "Eye Contact," sermon preached on the *Day1* radio program, Aug. 24, 2008, retrieved from http://day1.org/1126-eye_contact.

34. Peter Van Dijk, "Professor of Happiness," *Ode Magazine* (Mar. 2008): 75.

35. William Rees, "Sorrowing Souls and Starry Systems," in *Pulpit Eloquence of the Nineteenth Century*, ed. Henry Clay Fish and Edwards Amasa Park (M. W. Dodd, 1857), 786.

Theme Index

Abandonment 44, 58, 106, 118
Abiding 20
Abundance 50, 86
Acceptance 36, 90, 106, 138,
    172, 174
Accusations 10
Action 18
Actions 178
Aging 120
Alone 28
Anger 10, 144
Anticipation 128
Anxiety 8, 58, 74, 122, 142
Appreciation 120
Arrogance 132
Attack 100, 144
Attacks 34
Attitudes 124
Authenticity 36, 46, 68, 132
Authority 66, 100
Awakening 76
Awe 42
Being Present 180
Belief 18
Belonging 20
Betrayal 72
Bible 6
Blessing 40, 48, 56, 90, 164, 170
Calm 168
Care 30, 92, 98, 104, 148, 158, 160
Celebration 62, 126, 154, 162
Change 60
Childhood 98
Choices 70, 106
Cleansing 88
Comfort 30, 102

Commitment 52
Community 48, 96, 146, 170
Confession 46, 68
Confidence 38
Congregation 146
Connection 116
Connections 44
Courage 38
Creation 12, 26, 32, 66, 82,
    138, 174
Crisis 28, 70
Death 54, 154
Deception 132
Dedication 114, 152
Defeat 100
Delight 52
Deliverance 8, 44, 48, 74, 94,
    96, 142
Depression 102
Devastation 134, 150
Devotion 114
Difficulties 164
Direction 112
Disappointment 72, 182
Disaster 60, 164
Discouragement 182
Distance 148
Distress 24, 142
Diversity 138
Dominion 12
Dreams 162,182
Drought 86
Encouragement 90
Enemies 100
Enrichment 86
Enthusiasm 184

Environment 26
Envy 64
Eternity 172
Evil 78, 178
Exhaustion 102, 134
Fairness 128
Faith 18, 98, 146
Faithfulness 50, 76, 112, 130,
    154, 172
Family 96, 170
Fear 8, 16, 30, 32, 38, 48, 60, 74,
    82, 122, 146
Fellowship 6
Focus 152
Foolishness 18
Forgiveness 10, 46, 68, 104,
    136, 166
Forgotten 28
Forsaken 28
Freedom 136
Friends 72, 96
Fulfillment 22, 52, 54, 108, 120,
    148, 180
Future 22
God 42, 48, 66, 184
God's Help 134
God's Power 150
God's Presence 110, 116, 140
God's Word 156
Goodness 130
Gratitude 130
Guidance 104
Guilt 46
Happiness 6, 56, 124, 164, 180
Healing 182
Help 40, 56, 158
Hindrances 152
Holiness 110
Homelessness 56
Honesty 20, 34, 36, 46, 68,
    118, 132
Hope 14, 58, 80, 84, 166, 182
Hopelessness 14
Humanity 138
Humiliation 94
Humility 68, 168

Hunger 108
Hurts 10, 72
Identity 36, 174
Idols 152
Impatience 100
Integrity 34, 36, 132
Joy 22, 62, 108, 110, 116, 126,
    162, 180
Judgment 128, 132
Justice 10, 14, 52, 78, 144, 176
Learning 114
Lies 10
Life 22, 54, 116, 120
Listening 112
Loneliness 28, 44, 58, 118
Loss 92
Love 50, 70, 90, 96, 130, 154, 172
Majesty 12, 42
Meaning 6, 54, 64
Meditation 102, 156
Mercy 34, 166
Mindfulness 180
Ministry 56
Mistakes 136
Morning 124
Neediness 108, 176
Needs 30, 92
Obedience 156
Oppression 14
Order 66
Overwhelmed 24
Pain 134, 164
Panic 168
Party 126
Patience 52
Peace 112, 142, 168, 170
Peer Pressure 6
Personality 174
Perspective 130
Possessions 64
Poverty 14, 56, 64, 176
Power 42, 66
Powerlessness 38, 82
Praise 48, 50, 62, 76, 88, 124, 126,
    130, 140, 146, 148, 184
Prayer 122, 166, 178

Pride 14
Priorities 130
Promise 164
Prosperity 14
Protection 8, 16, 24, 30, 40, 60, 74, 82, 92, 122, 158, 160
Provision 86, 92, 150, 158, 172
Punishment 144
Purity 88, 156
Purpose 22, 54
Pursuing God 114
Quiet 60, 84, 168
Reaction 80
Reality 36, 116
Redemption 104, 106, 116
Refuge 24, 50, 84
Relationships 20, 72, 118
Remembering 102
Rescue 94, 172
Response 80
Responsibility 12, 26
Rest 30, 84
Restoration 30
Revenge 144
Righteousness 16, 18, 20, 34, 78, 128, 176, 178
Safety 8, 32, 60, 122
Salvation 106
Sanctuary 110
Satisfaction 108, 120
Security 8, 16, 32, 52, 122
Seeking God 156
Serenity
Sexuality 174
Shame 10, 34, 94
Sharing 90
Siblinghood 170
Sin 136, 166
Skill 104
Sovereignty 66
Steadfastness 70

Stewardship 26
Strength 24, 38, 40, 42, 70, 92, 140, 160
Stress 142, 168
Struggles 88
Study 156
Support 96
Terror 74, 122
Tests 88
Thankfulness 62, 76, 114, 140, 184
Thanksgiving 172
Thirst 58, 86
Thriving 86
Tradition 98
Transcendence 82
Trials 80, 88
Trouble 8, 80, 122
Trust 22, 32, 40, 44, 52, 70, 74, 80, 84, 94, 98, 100, 134, 140, 150, 160, 176
Truth 20
Turmoil 84
Understanding 148
Unity 170
Vengeance 78
Victory 62
Violence 78
Volunteering 56
Waiting 166
Water 32
Weakness 92
Wealth 64
Weeping 162
Welcome 138
Wisdom 18, 120, 146
Words 178
Work 162
World 26
Worship 76, 110, 126
Youth 98, 136